# Feel More Alive!

## 30 BRILLIANT WAYS TO REIGNITE YOUR INNER SPARK

## Giulietta Nardone

Text and artwork copyright © 2020 by Flaunt Your Difference, Inc. All rights reserved. All whimsical paintings strive to present subjects as a fantasy race. Author photos by James Tsakirgis. No part of this book may be used or reproduced in any manner whatsoever without the prior written permission except in the case of brief quotations included in critical articles and reviews. For information, address Permissions@CitrinePublishing.com. The views expressed in this work are solely those of the author and do not reflect the views of the the publisher.

Limit of Liability/Disclaimer of Warranty: While the publisher and author have used their best efforts in preparing this book, they make no representations or warranties with respect to the accuracy or completeness of the contents of this book and specifically disclaim any implied warranties of merchantability or fitness for a particular purpose. The author of this book does not dispense medical advice or prescribe the use of any technique as a form of treatment for physical, emotional, or medical problems without the advice of a physician. The intent of the author is only to offer information of a general nature to help you in your quest for well-being. In the event you use any of the information in the book for yourself, which is your constitutional right, the author and publisher assume no responsibility for your actions.

**Library of Congress Cataloging-in-Publication Data**
Nardone, Giulietta

Feel More Alive! 30 Brilliant Ways To Reignite Your Inner Spark

p. cm.

Paperback ISBN: 978-1-947708-25-9  •  Ebook ISBN: 978-1-947708-49-5

Library of Congress Control Number: 2020909053

First Edition, October 2020

 CITRINE PUBLISHING

Murphy, North Carolina, U.S.A.

(828) 585-7030  •  www.CitrinePublishing.com

For Jimmy

# Contents

# Visualize

# Express

# Self-Hope

# Foreword

*"Some people die at twenty-five and aren't
buried until seventy-five."*
~ Benjamin Franklin

"FIND YOUR GROOVE. *Follow your passion. Live your best life.*"
Self-help messages like these bombard us endlessly,
delivered by books, magazines, blogs, and omnipresent social
media. Yet these enthusiastic mantras often backfire.

Why?

Few of us have the time, income, know-how, or drive to
attend regular wellness retreats in the Colorado Rockies.
We can't just quit our jobs and support ourselves by selling
homemade pottery. Struggling to meet the demands of work,
parenting or caring for elders, or finding ourselves otherwise
caught up in the increasingly frenetic pace of modern life,
it's tough for many of us even to imagine what "living our

best life" means. The pressure to envision and then create that serene alternate existence can result in new forms of pressure, overwhelm, and dissatisfaction, leaving many of us feeling less hopeful than ever.

Even so, many of us really do want to change our lives, whether by engaging with the world in new ways, or by reconnecting with our deepest truths. Yet despite what many self-help gurus profess, change isn't simple. It's difficult, a mountain so formidable, few have the courage to scale it.

But why should that be? After all, an entire self-help industry exists to promote people's desire for change. Books and other media offer a dizzying menu of multipoint plans, research studies, mantras, and rituals, all promising to enable us to scale that mountain—right now.

Self-help, it turns out, has its limitations. Because so many models exist, we get overwhelmed. Many of those models encourage buy-in to an entire plan or philosophy. And when we inevitably slip up, or fail to follow through, we throw up our hands in failure and quit. Other times, we simply aren't prepared—logistically, emotionally, or financially—to commit to a total life turnaround. So, there we are, stuck at the bottom of the self-help mountain again.

I scaled that mountain. But not through self-help, and not by following the plan of any self-proclaimed expert. Instead, I discovered something better.

My impetus to change was the loss of something that formed the core of my identity: my voice. When I lost it, due to a rare condition called spasmodic dysphonia, I was told that this incurable neurological condition meant that I would never sing again. Even speaking would be difficult for me, a constant struggle to communicate. Faced with the choice of surrendering to sadness or finding fulfillment in other arenas, I opted not to surrender. Instead, I decided to embrace the cards I'd been dealt. I'd take on everything that came my way. I took up writing and painting, reconnected with acting, and involved myself with anything else that piqued my interest.

These actions did not involve ten-point plans or mantras. They were simple, concrete steps, undertaken with no specific plan to change anything about myself. I simply wanted to find joy in life again. But gradually, each small step impacted my life powerfully, in ways I could not have anticipated. Most importantly, they gave me hope. Hope that my life was not over, just because I could no longer speak normally or belt out power ballads at karaoke nights like I used to.

As I reshaped my life, I realized that change is not a scary external force, but rather a series of smaller, internal tweaks that anyone can implement without turning their lives upside down. Change with staying power comes not from following someone else's plan, but from within. It drives itself and becomes self-perpetuating, lighting the inner spark that for so many of us has dimmed or extinguished altogether.

Along the way, I began to call my process of change *self-hope.*

Maybe you've always thought of change as something meant to happen overnight, yet paradoxically also requiring massive, if not radical, life-altering action? (That's the way it is presented in many self-help books, after all.) And maybe just the idea of all that effort has discouraged you from taking any steps at all?

Self-hope offers something different.

*Feel More Alive! 30 Brilliant Ways To Reignite Your Inner Spark* introduces the concept of self-hope, a process of small, manageable steps that lead to a more inspired, dynamic life. Once you learn how to fill yourself up with hope, you can do anything.

The book is structured around thirty brilliant ways divided into five "ALIVE" sections illustrated with paintings— Awaken, Liberate, Improvise, Visualize and Express—to help reignite your love of life, no matter what challenges you may face. But I've learned the hard way that inspiration alone is not enough to spark change. That's why *Feel More Alive* also contains the concrete tools and activities you need to view change for what it truly is: an internal awakening, rather than an external altering.

The book in your hands is filled with short, relatable personal stories, each accompanied by doable actions. Because we all process information differently, I take a multisensory approach, reinforcing the main idea of each chapter with a tool kit of suggested supplemental books, movies, and songs selected to inspire you. The tool kits have not been endorsed by any mentioned writers, singers, speakers or actors; they are simply additional resources for you to explore after you finish each chapter. Songs get us in touch with our emotions; movies allow us to open our minds to new wonders; and books expose us to the wisdom of others. My goal is not to intimidate anyone with endless checklists, but to provide accessible tools you can easily follow.

*Feel More Alive* is different from the typical self-help book you may have paged through. It's not packed with research studies or vague language. I won't tell you to change your career or focus on making a million dollars (I promise!). You won't have to search these pages to unearth a buried nugget of practical wisdom. And this book is short enough for you to finish quickly—because I don't want anyone giving up before losing hope for a more zest-filled life.

Instead, I'll give you the practical tools you need to rekindle your inner spark and keep it burning. I needed a metaphorical kick in the pants to do that: losing my voice. But not all change starts with a dramatic, life-altering event. For most of us, it's simply a matter of realizing that we want something to be different. And my message to you is that by taking a series of small steps, life can indeed change.

Ironically, I find myself speaking up now, more than I ever did with my old "normal" voice. And people listen to me, even when I sound like a choppy mess. The small steps, and the small risks, I took after losing my voice allowed me to emerge as a more enthusiastic woman, the kind of person who makes "go for it" a motto. That capability was undoubtedly within me all along, but I'd never had a reason to dive within and escort it up to the surface.

It was because of this newfound confidence that I decided to try singing again. The instructor I found encouraged me to "sing up and over the cracks" in my shattered voice. So, I tried. What happened next is a story I'll share in later chapters. For now, as you begin this book, I want you to understand what it took me so long to figure out: transformation isn't the arduous task self-help books make it seem. And it doesn't require a miracle. Change is accessible to every one of us. We just need to be willing to "sing up and over the cracks" that trip up our lives.

Wishing you a life-sparking reading journey!

Giulietta

Awaken

# Brilliant Way #1

# Love Yourself

*"I have an everyday religion that works for me.*
*Love yourself first, and everything else falls into line."*
*~ Lucille Ball*

WAY TOO MANY FOLKS don't love or even like themselves.

I know, because I used to be one of them.

Ironically, no children are born disliking themselves.

That self-horror emerges along the way, with the help of adults and other children who've been indoctrinated to see the worst in themselves and each other. Instead of exalting the strength, the gift that accompanies every human being on this earth, we instead denigrate the weakness, fixating on the thing that does not make our hearts sing.

In my earliest years, I communed with nature. I thought I *was* nature. I took delight in the daily adventures taken around the neighborhood that was my tiny Garden of Eden. The tall white pines, the pussy willow trees, the dreamy meadows, the rock-faced hills, the lady slipper-lined paths, the gnarly tree branches, the sparkling brooks—I loved them all. I don't recall disliking anything or anyone.

Yet, that loving existence with myself and my beautiful world changed, perhaps imperceptibly, by sixth grade. By the age of eleven, I had grown to dislike my physical appearance.

Imagine an eleven-year-old girl trying to hide what she believes is a gigantic derriere by wearing her dad's large dress shirts. That was my new reality, my new daily goal. To camouflage what I had been told was an unsightly mound of flesh. When I look at pictures of myself at this age, I see nothing even approaching the derriere I imagined in the mirror.

Welcome to the world of body image insanity.

The big-butt saga was followed by the too-long-neck saga. Then the too-wavy-hair saga. Then the too-large-lips saga. Too-big-thighs saga. Too-small-waist saga. Too-small-calf saga.

My once theatrical, daring personality had been reduced to rubble by junior high because my reflection in the mirror didn't live up to the beauty ideal lodged in my own head.

In junior high, I'd be hustling from one class to another, when my legs would begin to feel like blocks of concrete that I could barely lift to move forward. I'd grab onto the lockers lining the hallway, pulling myself forward, hoping no one noticed my semi-paralysis. Looking back, I recognize that what I truly could not lift was my own self-loathing. It dragged me down, made me physically, spiritually, and mentally heavy. People said, "Oh that's just adolescence."

But was it really?

Or do we get parental and societal messages implying there is something wrong with us, or that we don't measure up to some narrow standard of beauty? If you watch Jean Kilbourne's powerful documentary series, *Killing Us Softly*, you may decide, like I did, that we're taught to loathe ourselves by people who loathe themselves, ad nauseam.

The heaviness in my legs (aka psyche) followed me into high school. Walking through the crowded, "cool kid" hang out/smoking area was like wading through a sea of molasses. Eventually, I started going around the back of the building, willing to endure getting scratched by a thicket of bramble bushes in order to avoid that psychological gauntlet. Oddly, I never experienced the heaviness of my legs when alone, only when in public.

My mental self-flagellation spread into other life arenas: relationships, work, and friendships. I floundered alone in a sea of people who seemed to have it together. My relationships brought me dissatisfaction. My work brought me angst and boredom. My outlook for a kick-ass, memorable life didn't look too promising.

So, how did I learn again to first like, and then love, myself?

Rather accidentally, I started talking to other young women. That's when I learned that most of us had self-love issues and body-distortion problems. Many young women, even those with "flawless" figures, didn't like their bodies any better than I did. Many found themselves in crazy relationships, where they, too, accepted crumbs of love, instead of the full loaf.

People who I thought had it together, confessed not only that they didn't, but also that they thought I did.

Once I realized that other women battled with their bodies (and minds), I tried to be more forgiving of mine. I tried to be less of a slave to my own internal query: "Mirror, mirror on the wall, am I the fairest of any at all?"

I got more in touch with the adventurous child within and ventured to foreign places, sometimes alone.

I accepted compliments. A guy I dated said, "You've got an awesome ass." Another commented, "I love your wavy hair." Ironically, these were the two features I had warred with most.

It took quite a few attempts, but I got the guts to tell my inner critic to "shut up." Once I got her quieted down, I had more room in my life to pursue things I didn't know I even loved.

I began to descend from the metaphorical bleachers and participate in the game on the field, slowly at first, then more. And more. To be clear: This did not happen in a week. It happened over a seven-year period, and only after I took small steps that connected into large steps.

I got myself a therapist.
I took acting classes.
I took singing lessons.
I took writing classes.
I got involved in my local community.
I joined a bike club.

I can now tell you that I love my wavy hair, my wit, my singing voice, my ability to encourage others to love themselves for who they are, my zest for life and, yes, most of the time even my juicy bootie.

Do I occasionally slip back into self-loathing mode?

Of course.

I'd be lying if I said I didn't. What's different now is that I've got the courage to rescue myself before sliding too far into the abyss of self-pity. I grab onto the sides and shimmy myself back up into the light.

You can, too.

# Way #1 Insight

It took a while to learn to loathe yourself. It is going to take a while to learn to love yourself and all the things that make you unique. Give yourself the time and space to do that. There will be ups and downs, but if you persevere, you'll get there.

~

# Love Yourself
# Tool Kit

**Song:** "Firework" (Message: You are worthy, valuable, talented.) Artist: Katy Perry

**Movie:** *Little Miss Sunshine* (2006). A girl who is unlikely to win a beauty pageant gets into the finals with the help of her dysfunctional family.

**Book:** *The Gifts of Imperfection: Let Go of Who You Think You Are Supposed to Be and Embrace Who You Are* by Brené Brown. Social work researcher Brown shares her ten guideposts for living and loving with your whole heart.

**Activity:** Every morning look into the mirror, find something to love about your face, body or personality and say, "I Love My Fill-in-the-Body-Part."

# Brilliant Way #2

# Laugh A Lot

*"I realize that humor isn't for everyone.*
*It's only for people who want to have fun, enjoy*
*life and feel alive." ~ Anne Wilson Schaef*

EVER SINCE I WAS a small child, I had a knack for making others laugh.

My family, my parents' friends, and the kids at school all found my impressions and one-liners hilarious. Only teachers seemed to immune to my comedic talents. I was stealing their limelight, and they didn't like it.

I've never forgotten the day in third grade, when a group of boys in my science class hovered around me and my pastel caricatures of movie stars.

We were all having a memorable time laughing together, the boys making silly comments about my subjects' exaggerated features.

Our teacher, Mrs. Leblanc, strode over and said, "Stop laughing and get to your seats." We ignored her and kept laughing. Naturally, she returned to the edge of our group and snarled, "Sit down now."

Again, we ignored her and kept laughing. She forced herself into our circle, shooed the boys away, and confiscated my paintings, which I protested. She ordered me to grab a stool and sit in the corner nose-to-nose with the ugly beige wall. A punishment she said for failing to stop laughing.

For. Thirty. Minutes.

The entire time I stared into the right angle, I thought, "Mean Mrs. Leblanc ruined our good time."

In fifth grade, I often traded comical barbs with Greg, another funny kid in my class. Our jokes sailed overhead, piercing each other like humorous arrows. As a result, we were usually sent out into the hallway to contemplate our "sins."

This pattern of being punished for causing laughter continued throughout my high school years, only confirming my belief in the necessity of humor. For my high school yearbook quote, I chose this from Victor Borges: "Laughter is the shortest distance between two people."

As an adult, I've noticed how many people never seem to laugh or have fun. They take everything too seriously, attributing false importance to their unyielding schedules, unbendable personalities, and unimportant job titles.

This approach to life makes no sense to me.

My happiest memories revolve around humorous situations: summer camp friends laughing over a silly punishment for not wearing socks to lunch; roommates laughing over chocolate, wine, and bad boyfriends; colleagues laughing over a supply budget so small, we foraged through the trash for desk shelving; neighbors laughing over the town government's evasions at public hearings; my husband and I unable to find a room in Budapest on our honeymoon.

Life is a lot more fun when you look for the humor. And much of the time, that humor is there, waiting to be discovered. Once you learn how to find it, you'll be able to use it to lighten up any situation.

# Way #2 Insight

Many people take life way too seriously. It is a more enjoyable adventure with humor as your companion.

~

# Laugh A Lot
# Tool Kit

**Song:** "I Love to Laugh" from *Mary Poppins* (Message: The more you laugh, the merrier you are.)

**Movie:** *This Is Spinal Tap* (1984). Hilarious mockumentary about a touring British rock band that plays at smaller and smaller venues.

**Book:** *The Laughing Cure: Emotional and Physical Healing: A Comedian Reveals Why Laughter Really Is the Best Medicine* by Brian King. Speaker and comedian Dr. King uses science to show the relationship between laughter and good health.

**Activity:** Gather some friends at home for a mid-morning coffee klatch. Toss out the question, "Anything funny happen to you lately?"

# Wander Like Leonardo da Vinci

*"Having wandered some distance among gloomy rocks, I came to the entrance of a great cavern...Two contrary emotions arose in me: fear and desire—fear of the threatening dark cavern, desire to see whether there were any marvelous things in it." ~ Leonardo da Vinci*

MUCH TO MY PROTECTIVE mother's dismay, I wandered as a young child. My ramblings took me all around my backyard, then up and down our street, then three or four streets away—and beyond.

It was the beyond that got me in trouble. My mother had told me not to leave the yard, but the urge to wander always overpowered the urge to obey.

I liken that desire to roam to being in a trance. Something almost supernatural seemed to beckon me into the unknown natural world surrounding my tidy suburban home. Sometimes it was the fields beyond my house that lured me. Other times it was the white pines congregating at the base of our hill.

Once, when I was around five, I took my little sister Joanne's hand, and we set off into the woods, crossing a stream and several roads, until we ended up in a cornfield backlit by the afternoon autumn sunshine. Just past the stalks of maize, I spotted a giant red barn. I didn't know what it was, but I was fascinated by the way the structure commanded attention, jutting into the sky.

The afternoon was turning chilly, so I reversed direction and dragged Joanne, who was whimpering at this point, back towards home. When we were just three streets away, my mother's blue Pontiac Bonneville station wagon careened into view. She stopped the car and jumped out, hugging us fiercely. "I thought you'd been kidnapped," she said, beginning to cry.

She kept a closer watch on me after that, making it trickier to escape the yard without her permission.

By the end of elementary school, my wandering was mostly confined to staring out the window. Eventually, my teachers put the kibosh on that with their edict, "Please stop daydreaming."

As I got older and more self-sufficient, it became increasingly difficult to suppress my urge to wander. But high school, then college, then a series of office jobs, confined me to chairs for long periods of time. Sitting for eight hours a day went against all my instincts. I lost track of how many times I went to the vending machine—not because I wanted candy, but because I needed to go somewhere, anywhere that moved my body from its unnatural seated position.

Every day, on my short lunch break, I ambled alongside a busy road, vehicle fumes spewing in my face. It wasn't ideal, but it was the best I could do, and it was better than not walking. Day after day, I bumped up against my unnatural boundaries like a wild animal caged in a zoo.

In my early thirties, during my two-week vacations, I started taking inexpensive trips to Europe, sometimes alone, to explore places I'd never been. Exposure to different corners of the world opened my mind to the idea of lifelong adventure. I developed a habit of always going somewhere new on vacation so I could see things I've never seen before. Then, when I turned forty, I read about the wanderings of Leonardo da Vinci in a book by Michael J. Gelb called *How to Think Like Leonardo da Vinci: Seven Steps to Genius Every Day.*

That's when it clicked for me.

From a young age, my curiosity had led me to wander physically and mentally, to collect new information and experiences, to expand my boundaries, and to generate new creative ideas. This exploration made me feel intensely alive. I realized that's why I found desk-sitting so painful. It interrupted the way I processed the world. To be truly happy, to find my way through life, to be fully human, I needed to be on the move. Exposing myself to new peoples, places, and cultures made me a stronger writer, painter, and graphic designer because I had reams of reference materials in my memory and imagination banks.

# Way #3 Insight

For a creativity boost, dedicate a few days a month to unplanned wandering without an agenda other than to explore. It might be somewhere new or somewhere old like your own backyard.

~

# Wander Like Leonardo da Vinci Tool Kit

**Song:** "Free" (Message: Wander to explore life possibilities.) Artist: Why Don't We

**Movie:** *Roman Holiday* (1953). A bored princess escapes her suffocating, sheltered life and with a companion wanders in awe around the streets of Rome.

**Book:** *The Wander Society* by Keri Smith. Wander to creatively disrupt your everyday life.

**Activity:** Wander the streets of a local city with no purpose in mind other than to explore. For an extra challenge, do not bring a map or a cell phone with GPS.

# Brilliant Way #4

# Share Your Tears

*"What makes you vulnerable, makes you beautiful."*
~ Brené Brown

How DOES A WOMAN get to her late thirties before she feels
strong enough to be soft enough to show her tender side?

Growing up, I learned to suppress my tears. My family
taught me they were a sign of weakness. My teachers banished
me to the corner for losing control. Eventually, I believed
that if I started I wouldn't be able to stop. Subsequently, I
summoned everything in my power to cut off tears at the
emotional pass. At the movies, I often hid in the bathroom
during emotional scenes, embarrassed to cry in public. When
I couldn't escape from my seat, I'd breathe in and out to hold
back the tears, or think of something funny. I'd dot my eyes

with my fingers or use a napkin to keep them dry—anything to keep other people from seeing me weep.

Years later, I was sitting with a friend at a coffee shop inside a large bookstore. A woman walked by who was at least seven feet tall. She was talking and laughing with her much shorter friend.

I'd never seen such a tall woman. *Life must be hard when you're that tall*, I thought.

But I continued to watch her, unable to look away, observing that she carried herself with grace and dignity and seemed completely at ease in her body.

My eyes welling, I turned to my friend. "That seven-foot woman is almost freakish," I said. "But she's more comfortable with herself than most average-size women, including me."

"I know what you mean," she said, watching me blink away tears.

Then my friend looked deep into my eyes and said something no one had ever told me. "It's okay to cry."

One grown woman should not need permission from another to express herself. I knew that. But after a lifetime of repressing my tears, my friend's words felt necessary, allowing a long-dammed river of emotion to flow freely at last.

For the first time in public, I cried, a salt stream cascading down my face and onto my blouse.

It felt freeing. Finally, I wasn't trying to hide or suppress one of the most human responses to emotion.

That's when I remembered Willie Don, my beloved quarter horse. My parents had given Willie to me for my eleventh birthday. A wild gelding with a big personality, Willie Don refused to be tamed by the world. Together we galloped through my teens, our long manes flapping in the wind. A year before I left for college, I sold Willie Don to another young woman because I couldn't take him with me. I wanted to assure myself that he would be okay, and to give him a final hug; but I couldn't bring myself to accompany my mother when she delivered Willie to his new home. I knew I'd be unable to hold back a torrent of tears, something I didn't want anyone to see, including my mother. So even though Willie had been a good friend during an oft-lonely girlhood, I never said goodbye to him. It was one of my biggest regrets.

That day at the bookstore, I felt like I was finally crying for not only Willie but also for all the other hurts I'd been accumulating inside.

Since that incident, when my friend sat with me, a witness to my sorrow, I have encountered many women in my writing programs who appear to be fighting back tears. Each time, I tell them that it's okay to cry, that they can let it go.

"We'll cry with you," I say, passing around the tissue box.

It's too bad that I have not been able to do this for men and boys. Maybe if I did, or we all did, there would be less violence in the world.

Maybe violence is nothing more than an inability to show one's true emotional soul through tears?

# Way #4 Insight

Stop fighting your tears. They reveal a hidden part of you that needs to be witnessed by others.

~

# Share Your Tears
# Tool Kit

**Song:** "Cry" (Message: Leave your heart open even after it has been broken.) Artist: Rihanna

**Movie:** *Love Story* (1970). A rich boy and a middle-class girl fall in love despite the misgivings of their parents. Life is sweet until the girl discovers she has a terminal illness. They cope with the upcoming separation as best as they can.

**Book:** *Crying: A Natural and Cultural History of Tears* by Tom Lutz. Eye-opening look at the cultural context of crying.

**Activity:** Write something that makes you sad and read it at an open mic night. Crying is okay.

# Brilliant Way #5

# Someday

*"Someday is a disease that will take your dreams*
*to the grave with you." ~ Tim Ferriss*

Do you find yourself telling others, "Someday, I'll go on that trip to 'fill-in-the-exotic-place'," or "Someday, I'll take that painting class"? And then, do you follow those statements with a sigh?

If you do, please pull up a chair and listen to me.

I spent most of my twenties vowing to do it—whatever that was—tomorrow. Before I knew it, I'd turned thirty, and I had done almost none of the things I told myself I would. I hadn't done X, or Y, or Z. I'd spent an entire decade doing nothing I could be proud of on my deathbed.

I faced a crossroads: stay on the current course, or get onto a different road and make things happen.

If I left my life on hold, waiting for someday to arrive, I realized, it might never show up. I moved my plan for tomorrow up to today.

One of the first things I did during my "turn someday into today" campaign was to take a trip to Italy. I travelled alone from Milan to Rome to Atina to Florence to Milan, staying in *pensiones* and the homes of friends of friends.

I danced in bars. I ate in outdoor cafes. I visited the Vatican. I viewed "The Last Supper." I marveled at the Colosseum. I got lost in the early morning fog in a tiny village. I visited my grandfather's hometown nestled in the Apennine Mountains. I got on a train hoping it was going in the right direction. I spoke broken Italian and ate gelato every day. I drove to Rome in a rickety station wagon with three strangers who spoke no English. And when a strike by air traffic controllers canceled my flight home, I stayed in a luxury hotel with six American soldiers and a gaggle of nuns.

I returned home a stronger, braver woman.

The next year I went to the Greek Islands alone. I came back even more brave.

Nothing is more life-affirming than taking emotional chances, I learned, because they are harder than physical or financial risks.

Had I waited for years to turn someday into today, it might have been too late.

We act as though our lives will last forever, assuming we've got plenty of time to do the one or two things we've always wanted to do. But we can never know how much time any of us have left on the planet. What can we be sure of? Today. And that's the best time to commit to something new. I've known many people who put off their dreams until they retired. Yet after retirement, those dreams were sidelined. Health problems and family commitments prevented them from realizing the goals they'd spent their working lives planning for. It's tough to hike the Appalachian Trail when you find yourself unexpectedly raising grandchildren, or tethered to a medical device.

These folks had spent their lives doing everything right: getting good grades, attending good schools, achieving professional goals. Life had been an orderly progression of socially sanctioned choices with a giant neon "someday" flashing in the distance.

We humans have been conditioned to be frightened of taking chances, trusting our guts, leaping into the unknown. Yet, life itself is a big unknown. So why are we afraid of the unknown inside the unknown?

It can be perplexing.

I am convinced that most strife in the world happens because people feel so bottled up by not taking chances that they explode in anger.

Who would want to do that, if they were living the life of their dreams? No one. They wouldn't have the time!

It can be difficult to step away from our conditioned routines. After all, they bring us comfort and stability. But they can also trap us into lives of stifling predictability. To override the fear of uncertainty, start with a tiny step. Sign up for a class. Try a new ice cream flavor. Ask someone out on a date. Every tiny step will build up your courage.

The size of whatever you've been putting off is unimportant. Taking action is what matters. Do it, whatever it is, so you don't reach the end of your life with more "somedays" than you have days left.

Life goes by faster than you could ever imagine. Go forth and seize the day!

# Way #5 Insight

Someday never comes. If you want to do something, instead of putting it off for someday, do it now because that is all you really have.

~

# Someday
# Tool Kit

**Song:** "Lose Yourself" (Message: Be brave and grab the spark of possibility.) Artist: Eminem

**Movie:** *Yes Man* (2008). A negative guy decides to take a positivity program, which encourages him to say, "yes," to everything.

**Book:** *Do It: Let's Get Off Our Buts* by Peter McWilliams. Encouragement to move in the direction of your dreams.

**Activity:** The minute you finish this chapter, put down the book and make a list of things you've vowed to do. Choose one and get the ball rolling on it today!

# Brilliant Way #6

# Embrace The Cards You've Been Dealt

*"You don't have a right to the cards you believe you should have been dealt. You have an obligation to play the hell out of the ones you're holding." ~ Cheryl Strayed*

I LOVE CHERYL STRAYED'S QUOTE.

It's easy to throw a pity party for yourself and bemoan the cards you've been given, instead of embracing those cards and using them to your advantage.

Cheryl's mother died young. She took her unbearable loss and turned it into essays and best-selling books. One of those books was made into a movie.

Reminds me of that saying to turn lemons into lemonade.

When I was a girl, I wished I looked like Marcia Brady, especially her long, straight blond hair. I spent hours smearing my hair down taut with goopy gelatinous products, trying to erase the waves. If it didn't look right, I'd wet it and start all over again.

If it had as much as a minor bump in it, I'd spin into a funk, often unable to leave the house that day.

Hours lost in front of the mirror, upset with unruly hair that betrayed me.

Then during one August lunch break in my late twenties, I got caught in an unexpected rainstorm, followed by a burst of humidity.

I raced into the work bathroom and saw a mess of out-of-control curls. All I wanted to do was hide in the stall until 5 p.m., but I couldn't. I had no choice but to go public with this insidious spaghetti on my head.

Surprisingly, the guys I worked with stopped by my desk and said, "I love your hair like that."

I thought they must be mad.

Then others.

Too many for it to be a fluke. As bizarre as this sounds, the comments of my co-workers woke me up to the beauty of my own hair, something I spent decades suppressing because it wasn't the hair I thought I should have.

At least once a week, people stop me and confide that they love my hair.

A few have asked to speak to me privately before spilling the beans. Others shout it out. Then there are those who ask how long it takes to create the waves and when I say, "it's natural," they almost get angry and say, "Don't tell me that."

I often feel like I'm traveling with a rock star on my head for all the attention my hair gets.

And to think, a summer rainstorm saved me from disliking a part of myself I'd been taught to loathe by others.

This takes me back to the wisdom of Cheryl's quote:

Sometimes what you thought you deserved wasn't even as good as what you already had.

We can get conditioned at young ages to lose all objectivity about ourselves and be forced into a perpetual state of envy, usually by folks who were conditioned themselves, and it keeps getting passed down through the generations.

I recall my fifth-grade teacher telling me my hair was too stringy and I should cut it. But looking back at the pictures it wasn't stringy at all. Her comments definitely sent me down the path of hair hatred.

If you ever succumb to the envy of others, make a list of all the wonderful things about you, large, medium and small, and frame it.

Here's to playing up the cards you were dealt.

# Way #6 Insight

Find what makes you unique and unleash it on the world. You've probably gone to great lengths to hide this fabulous part of yourself.

~

# Embrace The Cards You've Been Dealt Tool Kit

**Song:** "Defying Gravity" (Message: Be powerful and revered.)
Artist: Idina Menzel

**Movie:** *Legally Blonde* (2001). Dumped sorority queen follows her ex-boyfriend to law school where she discovers being too blonde is an asset.

**Book:** *Let's Pretend This Never Happened* by Jenny Lawson. Witty memoir about Lawson's unconventional upbringing.

**Activity:** Take something you've been hiding about yourself and share it with some of your close friends.

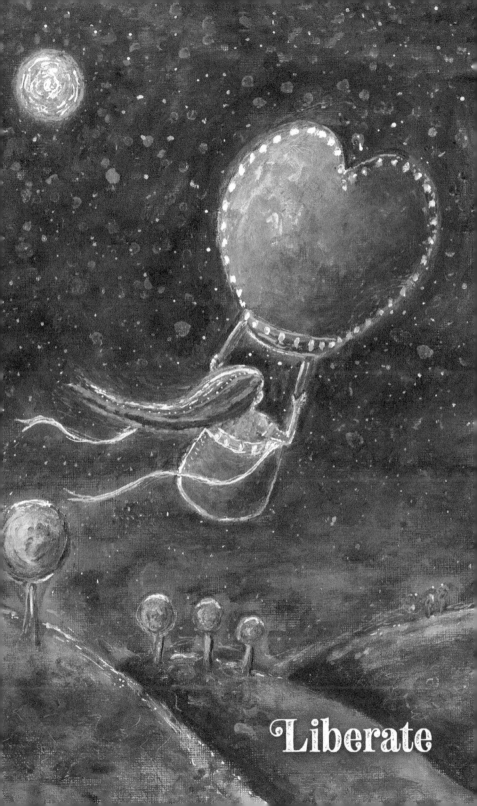

Liberate

# Brilliant Way #7

# Slap Yourself Awake

*"We live like zombies. We wake up, carry out habits
and go to sleep only to wake up and do it again.
You exist, but do you feel alive?"* ~ Anonymous

MANY OF US SLEEPWALK through our precious lives, lulled
by a false dichotomy of choices.

I know, because I found myself sleepwalking after I
graduated from college. My days were spent in a trance;
I was going nowhere in particular, doing nothing memorable.
Unable to get my bearings, I lived in a constant state of inertia,
fear, and loathing. I was jealous of people who seemed to be
loving life.

Of course, at the time I didn't know I was sleepwalking; I just knew that something was wrong with me, and I had to do something about it.

I tried therapy, and it helped a little bit. Then I tried another therapist, and it helped a little bit more than the first. Then I tried a third, etc. But what really helped wasn't conventional therapy. It was an ad I saw in the paper:

"*Wanted: stage hands for musical.*"

Immediately, I got in my car and drove to the theater. Thrilled that someone had showed up, the directors offered me the tiny job of curtain puller. I didn't realize a) how hard it would be to pull an antique curtain with my 115 pounds; and b) the importance of the curtain puller to the success of a play.

During performances, I used to peer out from behind the curtain and watch young adults my own age singing and dancing around the stage. One guy, Paul, struck me as odd but alluring. On my mother's advice, I'd always waited for guys to ask me out first. "Never, ever ask a guy out," she'd told me. "Or, he will not respect you." That message left me chronically waiting for someone else to affirm my worth. But I didn't want to wait for Paul.

One night after rehearsal, I gathered up all the courage I could muster and asked him out.

He said, "Yes."

My previous dates had always involved going to bars, followed by make out sessions in the front seat of my date's car.

Paul took me bike riding. It was nice to do something in the daylight. On our second date, Paul took me to a karaoke night. I listened in astonishment as he belted out a heart-stopping, Robert Goulet-worthy version of "The Impossible Dream." And as he returned to our table, after a thunderous round of applause, I felt a cosmic shift inside myself.

"I want to sing," I announced. That week, I signed up for singing lessons, and within three months I, too, was up on stage, crooning with the best of them.

"You have such a pretty voice," people told me. These compliments confounded me. Me? Yes, they meant me.

Decades later, I sing with a band during the summer concert series.

All of this happened because I saw a tiny ad in the paper and took a chance on answering it, instead of talking myself out of trying something new, as I so frequently did.

Back in 1854, Henry Thoreau wrote, "The mass of men lead lives of quiet desperation." That observation still seems to be true, over 150 years later. It applies to the life I was living as a young adult—before I decided to show up for my own life. I showed up for me. I showed up for something that made me feel alive. You can, too.

Remember to live the life *you* want to live, the life that makes you want to jump on the stage of your choice, pull back the curtain, and let yourself out.

# Way #7 Insight

Reject the early-life training that encourages you to put off living the life of your dreams until some fuzzy point in the future. To get yourself moving in a new brave direction, divide your dreams into big, medium, and small. Pursue some of the itty-bitty ones as a bravery building exercise.

~

# Slap Yourself Awake
# Tool Kit

**Song:** "Bring Me to Life" (Message: Wake up inside and be fully alive.) Artist: Evanescence

**Movie:** *Joe Versus the Volcano* (1990). A man diagnosed with an incurable disease and a soul stifling job accepts the offer of an eccentric billionaire to live like a king on a south sea island then die like a hero by jumping into the local volcano.

**Book:** *Wake Up and Live* by Dorothea Brandt. Proceed as though failure is not an option.

**Activity:** Join a local Polar Bear Club and run into the cold ocean or, if not that, a lukewarm lake.

# Brilliant Way #8

# Own Up To It

*"You can't go back again, even if you wanted to.*
*But you can own your own life, mistakes and all."*
*~ Ellen Barkin*

SOMEWHERE ALONG THE LINE while I was growing up, I started to lie when confronted about having done something wrong.

Looking back, I've come to believe that my impulse to lie stemmed from being punished by my mother when I admitted to minor household transgressions, like eating the last piece of cake or tracking mud into the house. Like any kid, I put two and two together. And what kid wouldn't want to avoid punishment?

Unfortunately, this behavior followed me into life beyond childhood. And in this, I'm far from alone.

We see it in the news all the time: Instead of forthrightly admitting, "Yes, I did this," a famous figure flatly denies wrongdoing. When the truth comes out months later, the person in question receives far greater public condemnation than they might have faced, had they initially admitted their misdeeds.

It seems rare for anyone to state the truth after committing a transgression, although exceptions exist. David Letterman comes to mind: He had the courage after cheating on his wife to admit his infidelity, apologize, and express the desire to move on.

I was in my twenties before I learned the power of owning up to my mistakes.

One of several female roommates in an apartment with a small shared bathroom, I had about fifteen minutes to multitask. I left the sink water running over some stained underwear and jumped into the shower.

Seven minutes into a shampoo and condition, I heard my roommate pounding on the door. "Stop the water! It's leaking into the landlord's apartment."

I pulled back the shower curtain and recoiled in guilty horror. On the floor, water stood a foot and a half deep. My underwear had plugged the sink drain and caused the water to overflow.

I scrambled out of the shower and used towels to sop up the mess and dry the floor as best I could.

Terror filled me.

I was going to get in big trouble. I'd probably be kicked out of this apartment with its reasonable rent. Where would I live? My roommates would hate me. On and on I ran through a series of disaster scenarios in my head.

When I emerged from the bathroom, my roommate told me that the landlord was sending a plumber the next morning. Could I let him in? "Sure, I can be there," I said, failing to mention that no plumber was needed, that the flood was entirely of my own making.

At work that day, I sat at my desk, unable to think of anything but ShowerGate. The tenets of Catholicism rippled through the guilt center of my brain. Should I let my landlord pay an expensive plumber to fix a nonexistent problem, or should I own up to my error?

Eventually, my guilt became overwhelming. Like the narrator of Edgar Allan Poe's "The Tell-Tale Heart," who imagines he can hear the pounding heart of his murder victim beneath the floorboards, I, too, felt I would go mad if I didn't confess.

My hands shaking, I called my landlord and explained what had happened. "I was doing hand wash and left the sink faucet on by mistake. It plugged up the drain."

Unlike my own mother, who often took a nutty when I admitted wrongdoing, my landlord remained calm. "I've done that before," she said. "Thank you for telling me."

Instantly, I felt absolved of my self-imposed sins.

Had I not found the courage to call, I would have spent the next couple of days terrified that the plumber would out me by informing the landlord the issue was "user error."

Surprisingly, no punishment followed. That emotionally corrective experience gave me more courage to own up to future wrongdoings.

Why cower in fear when you can confess in power?

Once you say the words "I did it," your accuser—who can often be yourself—loses power over you. You don't have to worry about your "secret" coming out, because it's already out.

# Way #8 Insight

Once I got over the fear of saying, "I did it," I took back my own power. The fear of "being discovered" can mess up your life more than the actual mess.

~

# Own Up To It Tool Kit

**Song:** "Your Life is Now" (Message: Take the high road and tell the truth.) Artist: John Mellencamp

**Movie:** *Liar, Liar* (1997). Attorney who has built his career on lying experiences a turnaround when his son's birthday wish comes true: that his father will cease lying for twenty-four hours.

**Book:** *Mistakes Were Made, But Not By Me* by Carol Tavris and Elliot Aronson. Highlights the human tendency to hold conflicting beliefs to justify one's actions.

**Activity:** Consider coming clean about something you've been lugging around in your soul. Start small and see how that goes. Then move on to something bigger.

# Brilliant Way #9

# Public Speaking 101

*"You can speak well if your tongue can deliver
the message of your heart."* ~ John Ford

THE TOP TWO REPORTED fears are death and public speaking.
Like most people, I used to share those fears. No one has
much control over death. But public speaking? That, I could
avoid.

Yet the more I avoided it, the more it controlled and
diminished my life, especially in school. Teachers had the
power to call on me at any time—or worse, make me come
to the front of the room and speak. It was one of the main
reasons I disliked school.

Nothing was more painful to me as a child or teen than
being made to give a report to the class. Lacking any guidance

in public speaking, I stood facing my peers without an iota of confidence. Would I say something stupid and be labeled an idiot? Maybe I'd be ostracized for speaking my mind. Or, what if I shared a story that no one liked?

Terrified, I used to fold myself down into my chair to avoid being called on, or pretend to tie my shoe until the teacher had picked her next victim. Only then could I sit up straight again.

In college, fear of public speaking determined my major. I combed through the catalog to discover which courses would require me to speak, narrowing my class selection to lecture-based classes where I could simply sit and take notes. If I attended classes in a potential new major, and the syllabus mentioned "class presentation," I dropped the class, even if I liked everything else about it.

Then, one day early in my junior year, I sat down on my dorm bed and read myself the riot act. "If you don't get over this fear of speaking in public," I told the scared little girl inside, "you are going to live a cowardly life." It took some self-convincing, but I made myself enroll in Public Speaking 101.

It didn't take long to figure out that every other student in the class was also terrified to get up and speak. Some almost fainted before their turn to stand in the front of the room. Others broke down with anxiety. Discovering that I wasn't alone in my fear propelled me to dive into it, armed with nothing but dry wit and the raw courage I was able to summon.

Fortunately, my imagination helped out, too, inspiring me to create presentations on how to steal someone's lips (you had to be there) or what to do if you have toilet paper stuck to your shoe. Before long, the speech professor was introducing me as the "girl who gives the funniest speeches on campus." That class kick-started a life of speaking up. Since then, I've seized the opportunity to do so whenever possible. I comment or ask questions at public events whenever I can. Standing up over and over has made me unafraid. I wish I could go back and tell my younger self that one day she would have the confidence to stand before anyone and speak her mind. Not even a condition that causes my voice to skip, rasp and crack can deter me.

If I can speak out, despite my mess of a voice, imagine what you can do with a normal one.

Free meetings happen in your town or city government every day. Agendas are posted, so you can find and attend meetings on any topic you feel strongly about. Most of these meetings are sparsely attended, and participants will be delighted to welcome you and listen to your comments or concerns. You can also join a local Toastmasters International Club and practice increasing your verbal boldness every week.

I tell every young person I meet to take speech classes. If you can persuade other people, you can change the world.

Once you get over your fear of speaking before others, you'll jump at the chance to sprint to the front, because you'll love the feeling of owning the room.

Dive into any fear and it will disperse.

# Way #9 Insight

If you fear speaking up, do everything in your power to overcome it. Those who speak up rule not only the world, but also their own lives.

~

# Public Speaking 101
# Tool Kit

**Song:** "Brave" (Message: Speak your truth and be seen.)
Artist: Sara Bareilles

**Movie:** *Braveheart* (1995). A medieval Scottish rebel tries
to free Scotland by fighting a tyrannical English ruler. In a
famous battleground speech, he inspires his reluctant army
to stand up and fight for their freedom.

**Book:** *Steal the Show: From Speeches to Job Interviews to
Deal-Closing Pitches, How to Guarantee a Standing Ovation
for All the Performances in Your Life* by Michael Port.
Performance strategies to own the room.

**Activity:** Go to the community participation section of
your local Town Hall meeting. Express a concern or make
a comment.

# Brilliant Way #10

# Do Nothing

*"Beware the barrenness of a busy life."*
*~ Socrates*

I FIRST BECAME AWARE OF the culture of busyness as a young adult.

"How are you?" I'd ask friends or acquaintances.

"Busy."

Being super busy had somehow become synonymous with living a full adult life, it seemed. Kids had to be increasingly busy as well, I noticed, dashing from one sporting event to the next college application-worthy activity, all in an effort to prove themselves well-rounded, popular with their peers, and destined for greatness.

When I was growing up, my parents and I ate dinner together every night. Eventually, the overscheduling craze obliterated that ritual for the families I knew, replacing it with burgers and fries grabbed on the run.

This veneration of busyness confounded me. I participated in plenty of activities, from singing to hiking to biking. But balancing those interests with quiet downtime came naturally to me.

Nevertheless, a part of me couldn't help wanting to be a card-carrying member of the busyness brigade, a winner who lived her life on fast forward.

*Why can't I be insanely busy like everyone else?* I'd wonder. *What's wrong with me?*

*How can I squeeze more into my life?*

It never occurred to me that the people whose bustling lives I admired were really just busy being busy—or, worse, pretending to be busy when they weren't, in an attempt to convince themselves and others they were leading full, meaningful lives.

It was a common mistake for a young person just beginning to establish herself in the adult world: measuring myself against someone else's life, without knowing the details of that life.

Assuming that those frenetic lives were better than mine, I tried to embrace the lifestyle. Soon I, too, was responding, "Busy!" when anyone asked about me.

Yet the more I tried to overfill my life, the emptier it became. Trying to keep up with the busy Joneses extracted an unanticipated price: the increasing sense that I wasn't doing enough.

Rush, rush, rush. To nowhere.

It was only after being laid off with even more time on my idle hands that I was able to reject the culture of busyness and reconnect with the core values I'd suppressed for too long. Now, once again, I began to embrace rest, relaxation, and rejuvenation as necessary for physical, emotional, and artistic health.

I watched dogs frolicking at the park. I listened to birds chirping in my backyard. I chatted about life with my older neighbor on the corner bench at the intersection. And as much as possible, I chilled on the couch with my two cats purring by my side. No music. No TV. No Internet.

Some might label what I was doing meditation; but even that term can feel like a do-something action, intended to transport me from here to there.

Nope. I was simply doing nothing. The Italians call this *dolce far niente*: sweet idleness.

Afraid to be alone with ourselves, many of us hide behind busyness. Perhaps we fear quiet, which may force us to confront thoughts we'd rather push away. So, we keep ourselves in a perpetual state of frenzy, which amps up the fear of self-awareness, producing stress.

Yet after abandoning my brief foray into the land of busy, stress has largely vanished from my life. For me, stress resulted from the perceived gap between the life I thought I should lead and the one I was actually leading.

It is far more calming to appreciate the riches I already possessed.

# Way #10 Insight

Take time every day to be idle, unproductive, to drift.

~

# Do Nothing
# Tool Kit

**Song:** "Sitting on The Dock of The Bay" (Message: Be at peace with the rhythms of life.) Artist: Otis Reading

**Movie:** *Enchanted April* (1991). A slow-paced story about four women who rent a villa for a month on a remote Italian Island to reassess their hectic lives.

**Book:** *The Art of Doing Nothing: Simple Ways to Make Time for Yourself* by Veronique Vienne. Positive suggestions to reduce stress and enjoy life!

**Activity:** Take a nap in the middle of the day.

# Brilliant Way #11

# Travel Light

*"Travel light, live light, spread the light, be the light."*
~ Yogi Bhajan

THE FIRST TIME I went to Italy, I brought a purse, a knapsack, a large suitcase, and a garment bag. My trip would last two weeks, and I still wondered if I had packed enough.

Bringing too much stuff was a classic travel neophyte mistake.

I had enough clothes for eight weeks, and their care and custody weighed me down, literally and figuratively. Besides, I found myself wearing the same couple of pants and blouses over and over. The rest of my massive wardrobe lay undisturbed.

To get around in Italy, I shared crowded trains with hordes of savvy backpackers. Most were Australians who had been trekking across Europe for months. More times than I care to admit, I found myself cursing, kicking, and castigating my bags. I wanted them and their inconvenient, unnecessary weight gone from my trip.

I envied the Aussies' minimalist approach to sightseeing. For them, it was all about the trip, not the luggage.

After four days, I'd had enough. I got a big box, stuffed it with the contents of my garment bag and, at great expense, shipped it home to Massachusetts, vowing to bring half as much on my next trip.

Had I not downsized my wardrobe, the stress of juggling it all would have ruined my trip. Lightening my load made it easier for me to get to the destinations I'd flown 4,000 miles to see and to be more upbeat in my attitude. After all, I was here to have fun, too.

Thankfully, I returned home with an Italian sensibility, a newfound buoyancy, and an appreciation for a more minimalist lifestyle.

At home, I continued downsizing my fashion load. Instead of constantly shopping for new outfits to wear at work, I rotated five, using my new free time to take up biking, a method of transport that would propel my husband and me across Italy several decades later.

It wasn't always easy to stop shopping. But in the process of inspecting my lifestyle through an Italian lens, I realized that I'd been using shopping as an excuse to live a superficial life. It was far easier to hide in the mall on weekends than to hurl myself into fired-up living.

And after that Italian trip, it also occurred to me that at the end of my life, I'd be comforted not by memories of clothes that had filled my closet, but by the adventures that filled my heart and soul: staring in awe at the Statue of David, gazing at the purple Apennine mountains surrounding my grandfather's birthplace; or savoring a glass of wine under a red Tuscan sun.

## Way #11 Insight

Figure out what you really need to have a good life, not what you've been told you really need. Get rid of the rest. You'll feel lighter and less burdened as you travel through life.

~

# Travel Light
# Tool Kit

**Song:** "Travelin' Light" (Message: Travelin' light makes it easier to soar.) Artist: Eric Clapton

**Movie:** *Tracks* (2013). Young woman leaves everything behind and undertakes a 1,700-mile journey across the deserts of Western Australia with four camels and her dog.

**Book:** *Repacking Your Bags: Lighten Your Load for the Good Life* by Richard Leider and David Shapiro. Leave behind what no longer works in your life.

**Activity:** Take a day trip with nothing but your wallet.

# Brilliant Way #12

# It's Only A Movie

*"Stop fighting yourself and start fighting for yourself."*
~ *The Revolutionary Impact*

DURING THE FOURTEEN YEARS I worked for The Man, I suffered through a lot of crazy bosses. To their credit, these were people with good intentions. But they seemed ill-suited to lead, encourage, and inspire others. Often, I'd escape from one position only to discover that my new boss was even worse than the old one.

My working life felt a little like being trapped in the movie *Groundhog Day*, where every day I woke up to live over and over the same frustrating work experience.

Mercifully, I had two good bosses in my life. One of them, Mike, uttered one of the most profound bits of advice I've ever encountered in a "work-for-someone-else" environment. It happened after I'd gotten myself into yet another snit over changing expectations for a research study I'd been managing.

"They keep changing the study's variables on me," I told Mike, exasperated. "I have to keep going back into the field to ask subjects additional questions. I'll never meet the deadline."

"Don't get yourself too worked up," said Mike. "It's only a movie."

I stared at him. "What's only a movie?"

"Life."

As I stood there, at a loss for words, I realized for the first time in my life that most of my routine workplace frustrations wouldn't matter in the larger scheme of life. Heck, they wouldn't even matter a year from now.

That was when I began to actively unlearn the bad training I'd received over the previous decades. Every time I started to freak out at work about something over which I had little control, I closed my eyes and chanted Mike's wise words: "It's only a movie. It's only a movie. It's only a movie."

His mantra freed me from my previous go-to emotions in those situations: frustration and self-castigation. Now I understood that I had the power to emotionally walk away from the pretend work movie set anytime I wanted, leaving me better able to function in its physical realm.

And I did. And I do. With Mike's help, I decided for myself that a lot of my work angst was a choice. And I didn't have to make that choice. Are there some situations where people may have less of a choice than I did to walk away? Absolutely. Everyone must decide what is in their own best life interest.

For me, I chose to stop trying to control the uncontrollable, which was just about everything. I chose to talk myself down from the ledge, knowing that much of the time I put myself up there. I chose to take a breath and observe the situation from a different vantage point.

"Am I really on a ledge or do I just think I'm on a ledge?"

A few days after being unexpectedly laid off from a union job, I was offered the opportunity to take the next lower position—by bumping out the current occupant. The Human Resource folks explained to me this was an acceptable practice and then the person I bumped could turn around and bump the person under them. The previously fearful me most likely would have pushed someone else out of a job to save her own. The new brave me decided to take her chances in an uncertain job market. Within four weeks, I had a more interesting, higher-paying job at a company closer to my home.

Instead of training everyone at an early age to be afraid of the unknown, why not encourage them to move toward it? To see uncertainty as the ultimate life high? The road to freedom? The path to aliveness?

Regrettably, I never got a chance to tell Mike how many times his words had saved me from the deranged clutches of my own work-induced emotions. One winter day, he slipped on a patch of ice, hit his head, and died.

Mike, if you're listening from wherever angels tread, thank you for being a voice of reason in a sea of job insanity. You were a great boss, and I will always remember how you helped save my work life.

# Way #12 Insight

Many of us can create crazy work situations in our head that may not exist anywhere else and then react to them. Reduce feelings of powerlessness by writing a new script that puts you in a position of power over yourself.

~

# It's Only A Movie
# Tool Kit

**Song:** "Don't Worry Be Happy" (Message: It's going to be alright.) Artist: Bobby McFerrin

**Movie:** *The Matrix* (1999). Man lives two lives. By day he is a computer programmer. By night he is a hacker who questions his reality.

**Book:** *Victim of Thought* by Jill Whalen. We are not our thoughts.

**Activity:** The next time you feel stressed at work, stop and ask yourself, "Is this thought real?"

Improvise

# Brilliant Way #13

# Stayin' Alive

*"I don't believe people are looking for the meaning
of life as much as they are looking for the experience
of being alive."* ~ Joseph Campbell

IN THE MOVIE *Saturday Night Fever*, Bobby, the most awkward and lost of Tony Manero's friends, falls or "jumps" off the Verrazzano-Narrows Bridge in Brooklyn.

When a police officer asks if Bobby intentionally killed himself, Tony's response echoes the idea that there are ways people can kill themselves without actually committing suicide.

That scene was the moment when I realized this was more than a dance movie.

After each week of dead-end work at the hardware store, Tony comes alive on the disco floor, completely in the zone, commanding everyone's attention. You can't take your eyes off him. He is on fire.

*Saturday Night Fever*'s message still resonates: Find the thing in life that makes you feel alive, and do it as much as you can. Then, no matter how mundane your day-to-day circumstances, your life will have meaning, movement, and magic.

What makes us feel alive? That will be different for each of us. Sometimes we know it intuitively. Other times, we have to search for it. Occasionally, we stumble on it by accident.

"It's a shame," said my husband, Jimmy, after work one day. "But they're going to tear down our town's historic Town Hall."

"Which building is that?" I asked, oblivious to my own town's history.

"The elegant white one in the center of town. It's got to be at least 150 years old."

Abashed that I'd never noticed something my husband obviously admired, I asked him to take me to see it. That afternoon we drove into town to look at the pre-Civil War structure.

Jimmy took me around the perimeter and pointed out the ornate detail work, explaining that it was camouflaged by the white paint and trim.

Immediately, I fell in love with the building. I, too, was

struck by the local history it represented and the lives that worked together to create it. This defenseless antique needed someone to fight for it, someone to push back against the modernizing forces who wanted to tear it down. So, I got involved. For the next four years, I worked with others to save, then rehab, the historic beauty.

When we finally unveiled the restored building, a reception of 300 excited people proclaimed to one another, "It's the prettiest Town Hall in Massachusetts." Before I got involved in the fight to save the Town Hall, I'd never stood up for anything, let alone myself. But once I woke up to my own power and ability to effect change, I continued to speak up about all sorts of injustices.

If Jimmy hadn't come home that day and mentioned the Town Hall's imminent destruction, I'm not sure the power within me would have been actualized. After sleepwalking through my adult life for so long, I needed something to wake me up, to pull me out of my involuntary hibernation, and push me back into the world of the fully living.

We all need a reason to get up in the morning, something that drives us to be the best version of ourselves, that gives us a reason to fall in love with our own lives. I found mine waking others to their own power. You can find yours by immersing yourself in new pursuits. Notice which activity makes you feel so powerful, so good, so purposeful, that you can't stop doing it.

Do more of that.

# Way #13 Insight

At least once in our lives, we are presented with the opportunity to embark on a heroic journey, an adventure that will transform us into a more powerful, fully alive version of ourselves. Most of us will turn down this call to action, afraid that fulfilling it is impossible. But when we persevere despite our fears, our lives become immeasurably enriched.

~

# Stayin' Alive
# Tool Kit

**Song:** "Let It Go" (Message: Discard your superficial shell.)
Artist: Idina Menzel

**Movie:** *Saturday Night Fever* (1977). A young man escapes his bleak everyday existence on the weekends when he dominates the dance floor at the local disco.

**Book:** *Feel The Fear And Do It Anyway* by Susan Jeffers. Confidence-boosting ways to change your life.

**Activity:** Go up to strangers and say, "I love my life!"

# Brilliant Way #14

# Leap Of Faith

*"What is the point of being alive if you don't at least try to do something remarkable?" ~ John Green*

My job as a research analyst bored me to tears. *I will die if I don't leave*, I thought.

One day, on my lunch break, as I walked around the park with a fairly new colleague, I confessed my need for greater challenges. "Quit without another job," he advised. "It will be the most liberating thing you ever do."

I stopped in my tracks. *Quit? No other job? That's dumb advice*, I thought.

I'd been trained to go from one full-time job to the other and avoid getting fired. If I got laid off, I hustled 24/7 until I got another. Only losers had medium-to-long stretches of unemployment, I believed. The thought of taking this leap was crazy. I could imagine my jobless self only too easily: living in a shabby shanty, no food to eat, my clothes torn, my hair matted. I might never be hired again!

Until my colleague shared that advice, I'd never questioned my beliefs about continuous full-time employment, or where they came from. Yet I kept mulling over what he had said, weighing his counsel against my own need to feel financially safe. I did have a little money put away in the bank, I reminded myself. It wasn't a lot, but it would last six months. Wasn't this the type of thing savings accounts exist for?

I needed to take a chance on my employment life. For. Once.

Three months later, I gathered up my courage and gave notice. After quitting, I took graphic design classes and embarked on a freelance journey—destination unknown.

In the months that followed my departure, I met two different types of people. Some thought I had made a big mistake; others called me courageous and said they wished they had the *chutzpah* to do the same thing.

Looking back, I can't understand why I was so terrified to leave a job without another one lined up. It was just a job. There'd be more.

But what I couldn't get was another life. This was my one and only, so why fritter it away in a place I no longer enjoyed, doing something that didn't feed my current soul?

I decided I wasn't going to take just any new job that I found, something I'd done in the past. I didn't want to find myself in the same boat I'd just jumped out of.

I met with a recruiter and told her what I wanted: a great boss, flexible hours, and the power to mold the job to my own strengths. Without missing a beat, she said, "If I find a job like that, I'm going to take it."

Bad fit.

I found a different recruiter and gave her the same list of must-haves. "Let's try," she said. Within two months, she found me the job of dreams. It was in a completely different field, with higher pay, flexible hours, and a supportive, terrific boss who told me, "Absolutely, mold the job to your strengths."

I had visualized what I wanted, believed it existed, and voilà! It had appeared.

When I shared my success story with friends, they often told me that they would definitely do something similar. They were going to leave their corner offices, not wanting to get stuck there for life.

"You won't regret it," I told them.

Fifteen years later, many of those friends are still in those offices. "They gave me a raise," one explained. Another told me, "I only have ten more years to retirement." Said a third, "My kid is in college."

Why the fear? Why the inability to believe that we will end up in a better place? Why the decision to take the road more travelled? I believe it all stems from our societal conditioning to make the safe choices. But safe choices never lead to a kickass life.

That first leap of faith I made was not easy. It took courage to overcome my lifelong impulse to follow the safe, societally sanctioned path. But that first leap of faith has allowed me to take many others over the years.

I've never regretted any of them.

# Way #14 Insight

If you want to do something but feel afraid, do it anyway.

~

# Leap Of Faith
# Tool Kit

**Song:** "A Change Would Do You Good" (Message: Change it up and see what happens.) Artist: Sheryl Crow

**Movie:** *Wild* (2014). To both heal and find herself, a recently divorced young woman hikes 1,100 miles along the Pacific Coast Trail after the loss of her beloved mother.

**Book:** *The Universe Has Your Back* by Gabrielle Bernstein. Move through life focusing on love rather than fear.

**Activity:** Pick a leap of faith you would like to take and announce it publicly. Announcing it gives it life.

# Brilliant Way #15

# Astonish Yourself

*"High expectations are the key to everything."* ~ Sam Walton

WHEN I FIRST BECAME a karaoke singer, I stuck to songs written in the safe middle range, neither too low or high.

My voice sounded decent. People applauded my performances and even stopped me on the way to the ladies' room afterwards to compliment my pretty voice. I enjoyed the praise lavished on me by fellow patrons, but I wasn't challenging myself.

Frankly, I didn't have the guts to sing these soaring ballads by Whitney Houston or Donna Summer that would demand more of me. *What if my voice cracked? What if no sound at all came out?* The potential for embarrassment kept me cranking out my dull, but comfortable, repertoire.

One autumn night, I went to karaoke alone. After singing three of my regular numbers, I finished my glass of Chardonnay and headed toward the exit. A young woman who was laughing with her friend in the smoking area approached me. "I love your voice," she said. "But, do you mind if I tell you something?"

"No, please do," I said.

"You can sing way more powerful songs, ones that will showcase your talent."

I was astounded that a stranger had called me out on my own fear.

On the drive home, I replayed her words over and over. The stranger was right. I'd been limiting myself to get the guaranteed applause instead of challenging myself to win my own acclaim.

I'd also lived with a rare voice condition that had robbed me of my speaking and singing voice for eight years. A patient singing teacher and a lot of hard work had restored my singing voice. I'd been given a second chance at singing, so why play it safe now?

That night I made a pact with myself: I would spend the next six months going to karaoke every Thursday night, and each time I'd sing one regular song and two new ones.

It was the best thing I ever did for my vocal confidence. The pressure to sing two new songs a week forced me into song selections I wouldn't have chosen otherwise.

In a few short months, I was singing songs by the great Donna Summer and Whitney Houston, songs rarely sung at karaoke. To my astonishment, I almost never missed a note, no matter how high. And I rarely fumbled a lyric, even on a song I'd just learned. All those worries about bombing onstage had been creations of my own brain, in an attempt to keep me safe by singing small.

These days, I can sing almost any song, no matter how high the notes. All because a young woman I didn't know saw something in me that I couldn't see in myself. For that, I am forever grateful.

I don't know who she was, but I'd like to pay her deed forward and encourage all of you to stretch yourself: Do more than you ever thought possible.

What might that be for you?

# Way #15 Insight

Most of us rarely live up to our own potential because we are too afraid to try the thing we secretly want to do. We spend the rest of our lives filled with regret. But with a little bravery, we can accomplish just about anything.

~

# Astonish Yourself Tool Kit

**Song:** "Hero" (Message: When you are fearful, look deep inside.) Artist: Mariah Carey

**Movie:** *Gandhi* (1982). Man mounts a nonviolent civil disobedience campaign to free India from British rule.

**Book:** *Full Tilt: Ireland to India with a Bicycle* by Dervla Murphy. Way-off-the-beaten-path travel adventures.

**Activity:** If you want to do something, but fear you can't, say, "I can do this" and give it a try.

# Brilliant Way #16

# Forget The Outcome

*"Care about people's approval and you will
always be their prisoner."* ~ *Lao Tzu*

I SPEAK MY TRUTH IN town a lot, at small committees and
large town meetings. But that isn't the norm. Most people
want to speak but shut their voices down out of fear of
retribution. Frankly, they hold themselves hostage.

"They might do something to my property."

"If I need a permit for my addition, I might not get it."

"I'll be kicked off the committee."

Really? I've been speaking up for twenty years. Not once
have any of those things happened to me.

Most of us are less afraid of retribution and more afraid
of our own power.

If an issue keeps you up at night, and you want to speak out about it, you must do so—or it will eat you alive. That self-erasure will be far worse than any "retribution" from a government employee or anyone else you're confronting.

In my late twenties, I took an advanced assertiveness training class for women. The bold instructor had me sit on a chair in the middle of the circle, like a queen on her throne.

"What is your most pressing issue?" the instructor asked.

"A fear of speaking up," I said.

The instructor went silent for a moment and then said, "No. You have a fear of success. A fear of being powerful."

I sat silently, basking in the trainer's contrarian brilliance. Until now, other people had always told me I had a fear of failure. That assessment never resonated because I definitely tried new things. I just didn't take them far enough, or finish them. But this woman was right. I did fear success. My anxiety about speaking up was simply a symptom of that greater fear.

My instructor's advice? Divorce yourself from the outcome. Just do what you need to do, and worry about the ramifications later. And always speak up the first time. Never wait for a second opportunity because that will turn into waiting for a third and a fourth, until you never speak up at all.

It was the best wisdom ever passed along to me.

After I began speaking up regularly, I learned that if I say something, people may find fault with me. But if I say nothing, people may fault me anyway, for staying quiet. No matter which option I choose, I'll have critics. So, why not say what I want?

This epiphany freed me from the chains of silence I'd wrapped around myself.

Speaking up was a simple but liberating action, one I pursued with a sense of purpose.

Many years of learned wimpy behavior had to be unlearned.

I began with baby steps. I returned things to the store and asked for a refund. I told my boyfriend I didn't like the way he always picked the movie. I told my boss I wanted a small raise.

At first, it was difficult not to let myself worry about the outcome. These days, I don't give the outcome a thought. What might happen doesn't matter. What matters is that I am true to myself and what I believe.

Tell yourself, "I will not be silenced by voices that do not matter. I will take back my own power."

# Way #16 Insight

Critics show up, whether you say something or say nothing. Ignore fears of their condemnation. Say what you need to say.

~

# Forget The Outcome Tool Kit

**Song:** "Fighter" (Message: Adversity makes us stronger.) Artist: Christina Aguilera

**Movie:** *Erin Brockovich* (2000). Down-on-her-luck single mother of three takes clerk position in lawyer's office to pay the rent. She stumbles on evidence that helps win one of the largest direct settlement cases in history.

**Book:** *I Am Malala: The Girl Who Stood Up for Education and Was Shot by the Taliban* by Malala Yousafzai. The memoir of a young girl from Pakistan who spoke up and changed the world.

**Activity:** Find or organize a documentary movie group. Watch the movie and express your thoughts during the discussion that follows.

# Brilliant Way #17

# Start Your Own Small Business

*"Decide what you want, and then act as if it were impossible to fail."*
~ Brian Tracy

AFTER I GOT LAID off in my marketing communications job, I jumped into the interview waters and discovered it wasn't warm.

I had no idea that the landscape of work had changed so dramatically since the last time I interviewed. The work day had expanded from eight hours to nine. Goal setting had gone from once a year to weekly. How was a whimsical creative such as myself going to spend every Monday goal setting and every Friday goal achieving?

When I asked about flextime policy at interviews, I got a blank stare.

Fortunately, I decided to run as fast as I could away from those jobs. I took a chance and opened my own graphic design and writing company. To be honest, I didn't know what I was doing at first, fumbling my way through the world of owning a small business, learning as I went along. In an advanced logo design class I met other designers; we formed a support group and regularly passed along work to one another.

My networking group was helpful, but I needed something more. I saw a need for creativity programs encouraging people to get back in touch with their inner wildness; so, I designed a program called "Freeing the Wild Woman Within." Six brave women signed up, and each week, I led them through a different creative activity, from dancing to disco music to telling spontaneous stories with found objects. After the program ended, I created even more bold offerings.

My sister-in-law, who had a conventional job in retail, rolled her eyes in disbelief. "People actually pay to take programs like that?"

"Sure, why not?" I said.

You can create a business selling anything you want. Your biggest obstacle will be the people in your life who try to talk you out of it. "You'll fail," or "That is too risky."

Maybe for them, but not for you.

Let me share a secret: Selling is nothing more than spreading enthusiasm for your product. If you act like you are in love with your product or service, others will be too.

Opportunities live all around us, if we can just learn to see and seize them. Think of it as putting on a special pair of glasses that show the vast range of possibilities normally blocked from view.

Fear stops many of us from pursuing those opportunities. Fear can drive us to back to the conventional life dictated by others. The good news is that we can recognize that fear. It's the voice in our head that says, "You can't do this." When you hear that voice, run away from it as fast as you can.

Why?

Because it's lying.

You can do this. Set your sights on the "What?" and forget about the "How?" The voice asking "How?" is fear derailing your dream. Keep moving toward your "What?" propelled by your "Why?" and you will achieve it.

# Way #17 Insight

Decide what you want to sell and why you want to sell it. Then give yourself permission to do it. The hardest objections to overcome will be your own.

~

# Start Your Own Small Business Tool Kit

**Song:** "You Gotta Be" (Message: To succeed, you have to tackle life head-on.) Artist: Des'ree

**Movie:** *Joy* (2015). Divorced mother of three invents a new mop. On her way to becoming a successful business woman she faces betrayal, fraud, and trickery.

**Book:** *Side Hustle: From Idea to Income in 27 Days* by Chris Guillebeau. Step by step guide to launch an income-producing small business.

**Activity:** Make a list of things you are good at. Might be a service like teaching people to skate or creating a product like cupcakes. Share a flyer with friends and family.

# Brilliant Way #18

# The Little Things

*"Enjoy and be grateful for the little things in life, for one day you will look back and know they were the big things." ~ Robert Brault*

I KEPT MY CAT VALENTINO inside for the first fourteen years of his life. My husband and I lived on the edge of conservation land, and when we adopted the cat, we'd signed a waiver agreeing to keep him indoors. Most of the neighbors' cats had disappeared into the headlights of oncoming cars, or into the night screams of coyotes.

I agreed to the waiver, though I knew keeping Valentino inside went against his nature, which was to hunt and prowl around the woods. But he was our little furry baby, and I wanted to keep his adorable personality with us for as long as possible.

Then, when Valentino turned sixteen, I had a change of heart. He was growing old, for a cat, and it seemed to me that he had a right to experience the great outdoors while he was still healthy.

Soon thereafter, I put Valentino in a cat harness with a leash, and off we went into the wild suburban yonder. He made a beeline for the grass and promptly gorged on this giant salad bar for cats.

After stuffing himself with clover and flower petals, Valentino padded into the backyard and climbed to the top of our small hill.

We sat on the crest together, looking down at the house we shared. My husband and I had bought it because we wanted a large backyard, but this was the first time in seventeen years that I'd enjoyed the peaceful view from the hill.

Five minutes into our hilltop adventure, Valentino lifted his head to catch a soft breeze and turned to give me one of his kitty smiles. Soon I joined him in a facial wind massage. Nature's caress soothed me into a state of relaxation.

A year later, on what I suspected might be the last day of Valentino's life, I carried his ailing body into the back yard and placed him on the snow-covered ground for a final goodbye. He wobbled from bush to tree to snow patch, picking up speed until I almost couldn't catch him. Any worry that his paws couldn't handle the frozen ground dissipated as his paw tracks got further and further from the house.

My elderly boy, who knew nothing of cutting edge technology gadgets or consumer goods, showed me how to enjoy something as simple as putting my face into the wind, making paw tracks in the snow, or enjoying my own backyard. Leave it to an animal to show us humans what really matters in life.

Since those backyard walkabouts with Valentino, I've made it a point to notice the little things that surround me every day. People all over the Internet shout, "Go Big. Dream Big. Be Big." That thinking has its place.

It would be a shame, though, to go through life fixating only on the big things, when the little things are just as important.

Perhaps, towards the end of our lives, we will all realize that the little things were the big things.

# Way #18 Insight

Notice the small, wonderful things that already surround you: the inside of a flower, a friend's laugh, the symphony of birds in the early morning.

~

# The Little Things
# Tool Kit

**Song:** "Dayton, Ohio 1903" (Message: Stop to say hello.)
Artist: Randy Newman

**Movie:** *Wings of Desire* (1987). Two compassionate guardian angels observe the human condition on Earth. One falls in love with a trapeze artist and grapples with becoming human.

**Book:** *It's the Little Things… An Appreciation of Life's Simple Pleasures* by Craig Wilson. Wilson's words of happiness wisdom shared in a collection of nostalgic essays.

**Activity:** Sit in your backyard, front yard or balcony and tune into the tiny world percolating around you. Look inside a flower and you'll see a beautiful work of art. Listen to the birds sing and you'll experience a free concert.

Visualize

# Brilliant Way #19

# Meet New People

*"Encourage everyone you meet with a smile or compliment. Make them feel better when you leave their presence and they will always be glad to see you coming." ~ Joyce Meyer*

I USED TO BE TERRIFIED of meeting new people.

I didn't know what to say to strangers. Even if they asked me simple questions, I answered with curt, monosyllabic answers, my brusqueness masking a deep-seated fear of being perceived as a bore. Saying the wrong thing made me feel foolish. For me, these encounters were deeply painful.

This fear continued for decades—until I traveled to Europe alone. You might be thinking, what a bizarre adventure for a shy girl to undertake. And you might be right. But fate drove me to do it.

I had always wanted to visit Italy, my family's ancestral homeland. None of my friends could afford the trip, so I went alone. I planned to stay with an acquaintance in Milan, but by the time I arrived, she'd gotten a new boyfriend and shoved me out of the apartment picture.

It was time for Plan B. Unfortunately, I didn't have one. So, I improvised by taking a train from Milan to Florence to Rome.

All by my lonesome, barely speaking Italian self.

For the next two weeks, I stayed mainly in pensiones, the family-run guesthouses found throughout Europe, as well as with a friend's family in a tiny village. Not knowing anyone forced me to meet new people every day. Despite my limited language skills, I found myself asking for directions, making conversation at restaurants, and sharing laughs with others at tourist sites. I discovered that I was fun to be around.

When I got home, I continued my small-talk experiment, making a point of talking to people wherever I went. Now, instead of interacting silently, I chatted with the supermarket cashier, the bank teller, the woman using the locker next to me at the gym.

Did most folks seem to enjoy these conversations? Yes. Did a few seem annoyed? Yes. Did I let that bother me? No. I learned to roll it off my formerly sensitive shoulders.

If the holdouts wanted to move through life in a protective stance—the way I used to—that was their decision.

But my choice would be to say hello and make my world a friendlier place.

These days, I walk right up to people I don't know, extend my hand and say, "Hi, I'm Giulietta." Usually, they are relieved to have someone to talk to and if I'm on vacation, I find that most people enjoy the richer conversation and shared experiences that come from meeting other locals or travelers.

If you step into your braveness and connect with the people around you, you'll find most of them will love you for it. The key is to find common ground, which isn't that difficult. All you need to do is ask people questions about themselves such as, "Where do you live?" Or, comment on something happening in your immediate vicinity by relating it to pop culture: "I feel like I'm in a Seinfeld episode."

People love to talk about themselves! Once you find that source of connection, you'll soon realize it's easy to have conversations with just about anyone.

You'll feel empowered. They'll feel acknowledged. Everyone will leave the encounter feeling better.

## Way #19 Insight

Most people are as shy about meeting you as you are about meeting them. Break the ice by introducing yourself. Your reward will be a moment—or perhaps many—of enriching human connection.

~

# Meet New People
# Tool Kit

**Song:** "You've Got a Friend" (Message: Having a friend you can reach out to.) Artist: James Taylor

**Movie:** *E.T. the Extra Terrestrial* (1987). Young boy befriends a stranded alien.

**Book:** *How to Talk to Anyone: 92 Little Tricks for Big Success in Relationships* by Leil Lowndes. Commonsense tips and tricks to enhance communication with others.

**Activity:** Start a conversation with someone you do not know.

# Brilliant Way #20

# Wild Places

*"All the good things are wild and free."*
*~ Henry David Thoreau*

IF YOU WANT TO jolt your five senses back to life and discover a few more, visit the wildest place on Earth you can.

Make it far enough that your cell phone doesn't work and you don't have Internet access. That will force you to pay attention to your immediate surroundings. Your life may depend on it. And that's a good thing.

In 2014, my husband, Jimmy, and I went on a Safari to the Okavango Delta in Botswana, one of the last wild places on Earth. Within an hour of our small prop plane touching down on the dirt airstrip, we saw elephants, buffalo, giraffes, antelopes, and zebras roaming across the golden-grassed floodplains. If that wasn't "off-the-grid" enough, our driver stopped to point out a leopard napping in one of the trees.

We were visitors in a world ruled by animals.

Back at our tent with double bed, simple toilet and shower, we heard a rustling outside and opened the flap to see an enormous young elephant harvesting nuts from the jackalberry tree outside. He returned around 3:00 a.m. for seconds, serenaded by the grunts of several hippos wallowing in the nearby marsh. In the morning, we awoke to the trilled rhythmic call of the Cape Turtle Doves, short-short-long, short-short-long, short-short-long, a peaceful riff I grew to appreciate more with each passing day.

On our second night, I jolted out of sleep to the rumbling roar of several lions meandering through the camp in search of dinner. A visceral sound that left my nerves jangled but my imagination on fire. I was twenty-five feet from a creature that could have devoured me in seconds. For the first time in my life, I knew what it felt like to be prey in the crosshairs.

Toward the end of our five-night stay, Jimmy and I had been in bed for thirty minutes when he said, "I hear heavy breathing and pawing outside the tent."

"What do you think it is?" I said trying to envision what creature of the night lurked a few inches from our heads.

"A lion."

Honestly, I didn't hear heavy breathing but I heard something circling the tent, scratching at the thin canvas sides.

"Should we use the emergency foghorn?" I asked, remembering the staff carried no guns for the safety of the animals.

"Only if the creature rips through the canvas."

"Maybe we should do a pre-emptive strike?"

"Do we want to wake up the entire camp if we are wrong?"

Instead, we huddled together, motionless with at least me imagining the animal dragging my 120-pound body into the delta to be shared with a bunch of crocodiles and hyenas.

The excitement got my bladder going. "I've got to pee or I'm going to explode," I said.

"You can't. The lion will smell your scent and attack us."

Despite Jimmy's protests, I tiptoed to the toilet in our tent and peed as quietly as possible, hoping the urine smell would not waft through the mesh windows overhead.

When I crawled back into bed, Jimmy explained his newly devised Plan B.

"If the lion rips through the canvas, get down next to the bed and I'll pull the mattress over us, while you blow the foghorn."

I hoped it wouldn't come to that, but this creature continued to lean on our tent near our pillows, marking his property in anticipation for the marital kill. As horrible as it sounds, I wished for the animal to visit someone else's tent. The dog-eat-dog world had overtaken my sense of goodness.

I woke up five hours later with the sun's rays filtering through the mesh windows. Alive. Unharmed. Together.

Unable to stand the suspense, I said, "I'm going to check outside to see the lion's paw prints." I investigated around the perimeter, examining the layer of dirt with my glasses off to see better. No markings. Odd. How could that be? Did the staff rake around our cabins in the morning?

At breakfast, I mentioned the lions sniffing around our tent to the guide.

"There weren't any lions in the camp last night," he said "Must have been the wind."

"Jimmy," I said on the way back to the tent. "Do you think we were accosted by the wind last night?"

"No. It was a panting lion."

Whatever it was, my senses blazed with fire … and imagination and life.

On our return trip to the dirt airstrip, I waved goodbye to the wild animals staring at us as they munched on a grassy lunch or chilled under a tree. Something about the chance of losing my life made me appreciate it even more.

# Way #20 Insight

Our increasingly electronic-centered life can dull the five senses. To wake them up, spend time in a place where you cannot be followed by technology.

~

# Wild Places
# Tool Kit

**Song:** "Born to Be Wild" (Message: You were meant to be Wild. Go look for adventure.) Artist: Steppenwolf

**Movie:** *Into the Wild* (2007). Rich young man gives away his materialistic possessions and hitchhikes to Alaska to live in the wild.

**Book:** *Step Into Nature: Nurturing Imagination and Spirit in Everyday Life* by Patrice Vecchione. A guide to replenish your connection to the planet.

**Activity:** Go camping or hiking in the deep woods without your cell phone.

# Brilliant Way #21

# Starry, Starry Nights

*"For my part I know nothing with any certainty, but the sight of the stars makes me dream."* ~ *Vincent Van Gogh*

I'D SUPPOSEDLY "ARRIVED" IN society, and I had all the trappings to prove it: my advanced degree, my good-paying job, my loving fiancé, and my roomy apartment.

I had a bunch of nice possessions and the capacity to buy more. What I lacked was self-awareness. What was my place in the world? What was I supposed to be doing? I had no idea. I had traded a world of childhood amazement for a world of adulthood monotony.

My listless attitude improved one Friday August evening, when I attended an after-work party in a rural suburb. One of my colleagues, Heath, asked me if I wanted to go outside and look at the constellations. Not much was going on inside the crowded contemporary home. "Why not?" I said, although my status as a betrothed woman put me on mini-alert for any potential attempts at hanky-panky.

We strolled out to some lawn chairs and sat down. Heath pointed up at a thin line of light etched across the darkened sky. "What looks like a ladle is the Big Dipper; and over there, what looks like a W is Cassiopeia."

I gazed up at the gorgeous celestial display, trying to remember the last time I turned my eyes heavenward at night. Abashed, I recalled that it must have been decades earlier, during an overnight camping trip in New Hampshire.

I couldn't believe I'd lost touch with the humbling powers of the sky. Here was beauty I could gaze upon every night for free. All I had to do was turn off the seductive television and venture out onto my apartment's porch.

Soon after the party, I signed up for an online inspirational newsletter by Michael Bungay Stanier. In one of the first issues I received, he suggested that his readers go into their yards at night, gaze up at the sky with both hands raised, and shout, "How fantastic!"

Kismet beckoned and I gave it a try.

At first, I felt self-conscious shouting at the sky. To escape embarrassment, I checked to make sure none of my neighbors were outside putting out the trash or taking the dog for a walk. Thankfully, the more I practiced this nighttime gratitude call, the easier it got.

To this day, I still go out around 10 p.m. on cloudless nights and shout, "How fantastic!"

Besides making me feel good, acknowledging the stars helped me understand that I'm a small part of the giant universe, which is an unknown X that goes on forever, an entity I have no control over. Gazing regularly at the night sky has been a humbling experience, one that convinced me to surrender my desire for control. Once I did, I discovered I now had a new kind of control, the authority to let go of what I'd been taught life should be. "What's out of control is in control" became my new life slogan.

Whenever the desire to control something or someone infiltrates my brain, I let it fly into the universe, leaving me free to enjoy the magic of everyday life.

# Way #21 Insight

Put your life in perspective by looking up at the sky at night. It's a humbling experience that reminds us that, no matter what we think, we don't have control over much.

~

# Starry, Starry Nights Tool Kit

**Song:** "When You Wish Upon a Star" (Message: Wish and your dreams really will come true.) Artist: Linda Rondstadt

**Movie:** *Stardust* (2007). Teenager crosses over into the bordering magical land of spells, unicorns, and wishes to bring back a fallen star to the girl of his dreams.

**Book:** *The Glass Universe: How the Ladies of Harvard Observatory Took the Measure of the Stars* by Dava Sobel. Mesmerizing tale of women's contributions to the field of astronomy.

**Activity:** Stand under the stars, raise your arms, and yell, "How fantastic!"

# Brilliant Way #22

# Self-Educate

*"Catch on fire with enthusiasm and people will come for
miles to watch you burn." ~ Ralph Waldo Emerson*

Do you know what you love? How many of us lead lives
that are on fire, burning hot, full of passion and energy and
desire?

Judging by the volume of inspirational quotes posted on
Twitter, I'd say very few.

But don't most of us start out that way? Loving life.
Exploring environments. Asking questions.

Then we get sent to school, where we exchange dynamic
self-learning with static teacher-directed learning. Instead of
learning what we want to know, we learn what some faceless

curriculum specialist in a governmental corner office has decided we "should" know.

But who are those specialists, and what do they know about you, or your life dreams?

*Nada.*

It's all part of the current educational paradigm that believes everyone must learn the same things and become standardized humans. Many curriculum developers don't care, or overlook the fact that this one-size-fits-all approach makes people dislike learning.

Too often, when it comes to school, what students want doesn't matter—because our current educational model seems to be less about learning and more about preparing people like you and me to follow a prescribed pathway through life.

Yet after the grind of school is complete, we graduate into adulthood, free to begin our real education, the self-directed pursuit of our own interests.

Finally, we have the opportunity to gather our own fascinating kindling of subjects, build a bonfire, and light it with our own matches, instead of letting someone else light it for us.

Research some of the world's most successful people, and you'll find that many of them didn't finish high school or college. They had an idea they couldn't stop thinking about, and they pursued it with enthusiasm until it came to fruition.

In other words, they lit their own fires.

Included on this list are Richard Branson, Gisele Bündchen, Ellen DeGeneres, Michael Dell, Eminem, F. Scott Fitzgerald, Lady Gaga, Bill Gates, Steve Jobs, Ralph Lauren, John Lennon, John Mackey, Seth Rogen, Ty Warner, and Oprah Winfrey.

You can light your own fire, too. Just figure out what makes you burn hot, and pursue those things.

For me, one of them was investigating the stories my local government officials told me. They didn't make sense, so my neighbor and I started our own detective agency and called it "The Ashland Underground."

We attended a lot of public meetings, asked a lot of questions, made a lot of comments, and requested a lot of public documents. All the data was formulated into stories that shed light on the comings and goings of our local government. Then we took it one step further and launched a cable show for our community. We called it "What's Really Going On."

Our local audience loves watching it. And we love filming it. Being a minor celebrity has been a blast. Fans stop us all the time in the pharmacy, grocery store, or restaurants to tell us how informative, funny, and useful they find our programming.

Oh, and by the way, neither one of us studied journalism or television production in school.

# Way #22 Insight

Choose to educate yourself about topics that pique your interest. Read books, research findings, interview experts, and take informal classes.

~

# Self-Educate Tool Kit

**Song:** "It's My Life" (Message: Make your own breaks in life.) Artist: Bon Jovi

**Movie:** *Dead Poets Society* (1989). New English teacher uses unorthodox means to show his students the power of poetry and words.

**Book:** *The Teenage Liberation Handbook* by Grace Llewellyn. A life-awakening guide to the power and beauty of self-education.

**Activity:** Take a continuing education class on a subject you've always wanted to learn about.

# Brilliant Way #23

# Treat Every Day Like It's Your Last

*"Being alive is the special occasion." ~ Unknown*

GROWING UP, OUR LIVING room was off limits, except for Christmas and Thanksgiving.

My mother, a child of the Great Depression, protected the room's furniture and accessories with a vengeance. One day I came home from junior high to find my mother crumpled in a crying heap at the base of her expensive silk curtains. I looked up and saw my eight-week old kitten clinging to the top. Below her was a trail of nail holes in the transparent fabric. Mom's momentary nervous breakdown over a curtain panel seemed crazy. I vowed to never act like that.

Unfortunately, I did act like that.

Not with furniture but with clothes. Once, I found the expensive, white lace, bell-sleeved shirt of my dreams at a specialty store and stowed it away for safekeeping in the closet.

Sometimes I'd slip into it, dab on fuchsia lipstick, and dance in front of the bathroom mirror to Debarge's "You Wear It Well."

I radiated youthful beauty and confidence.

But at the end of the dance, the precious blouse went back into the closet, waiting for an occasion worthy of its promenade in public.

Parties and events would crop up. In search of something to wear, I'd take out the shirt and hold it up to my neck, admiring my charming reflection in the mirror. Still, the occasion never seemed special enough, and back into the closet it went.

Seven years went by, and I still had not worn the shirt. I'd almost forgotten about it, because it was now squeezed between other new clothes that I probably wouldn't wear, either.

One day I pulled it out for a family member's retirement party, deeming this, finally, a worthy occasion. Excitedly, I pulled the slim, fitted shirt over my head and down around my waist. I was going to look gorgeous.

Oh, no.

Looking in the mirror, I could see ripples of back fat through the delicate lace. It was now too tight. Over the years, I'd put eight pounds on my formerly tiny frame, and the beautiful shirt simply didn't fit my more mature body.

Heartbroken, I took the lovely shirt, its tags still swaying from the sleeves, and donated it to the Salvation Army.

Losing the opportunity to wear that shirt changed my outlook on life.

Henceforth, every day would be christened "a special occasion," and I'd wear all my new purchases within forty-eight hours. I did not have to follow in my mother's self-denying footsteps. I could, instead, follow the lead of my childhood kitten and use things as I saw fit, all in pursuit of a fabulous life.

Soon after I revealed my new life manifesto to friends, I bought a yellow lace raincoat and wore it the next day to a business luncheon. I bought a pair of velvet bell-bottom pants and wore them to a karaoke night. I bought a new vintage purse and carried it to a casual family dinner.

If I even thought of putting something away for safekeeping, I made myself put it on and wear it out of the house.

Now, when I donate something to the Salvation Army, it's because I've worn it out through love.

## Way #23 Insight

Stop savings things for that special occasion down the road of life. It never comes. Start using the things you love today.

~

# Treat Every Day Like It's Your Last Tool Kit

**Song:** "Live Like We're Dying" (Message: Do what you love while you have the chance.) Artist: Kris Allen

**Movie:** *Babette's Feast* (1987). Two elderly Danish sisters take in a French refugee to be their housekeeper during the Franco-Prussian War. Fourteen years later, she wins the lottery and uses the money to throw a feast to remember.

**Book:** *A Year to Live: How to Live This Year as If It Were Your Last* by Stephen Levine. Figure out what matters most in life and start doing it.

**Activity:** Take something you've been saving for longer than two weeks and use it today.

# Brilliant Way #24

# Monologue

*"Creativity requires the courage to let go*
*of certainties." ~ Eric Fromm*

MY TWENTIES AND EARLY thirties were a boring blur of
partying at clubs, toiling at dull jobs, and searching for Mr.
Right in all the wrong places.

Other twentysomethings in my circles also suffered from
chronic cases of ennui. We zombied around the music clubs
together, staying up too late and drinking too much booze.
No one seemed particularly happy.

*Is this all there is?* I used to wonder after waking up after
another drunken night of partying. *Because if it is, I'm not
sure I can take it.*

Every day felt like every other day. The drip, drip, drip of vapidness onto my soul.

A portal of opportunity opened when an unknown colleague left a continuing education flyer in the break room at work. I thumbed through the offerings as I drank my iced tea. Computer programs? Nope. Cooking classes? Nope. Makeup classes? Nope. Theater classes. Ah. Now those drew me in.

As a child and teen, I dreamed of being a film actress, and even had small parts in a few high school and summer camp plays. But after that, my dream was lost in the "grow up and get a career" shuffle.

"Acting for Beginners," an eight-week class, jumped out at me from the catalog. It took a few days to find the guts to sign up, but I did.

The class had twelve students and a knowledgeable instructor. We made funny faces and acted like animals, numbers, and vegetables. Then we moved onto improvisations and short skits, followed by a fifteen-minute play to be performed with another classmate.

The instructor paired me up with Laura and assigned us *The Faculty Lounge, Scene 5* by Michael Shulman. I played Rhoda Bootin, a shy southern mathematician reliving her first day at school. Laura and I practiced in class and during our lunch breaks at the gazebo on Boston Common.

In short order, I became Rhoda Bootin and talked exclusively in a Southern accent.

To this day, I can recite many of my lines. "Do you know that there are equations that make me cry?" "A phone call. I'm not very good on the phone. I get kind of nervous and people up here don't understand what I'm saying."

Our scene was a smashing success. "I didn't see you up on the stage," commented the instructor. "I only saw Rhoda." It was the best acting compliment I could have received.

Finally, I had a reason to get up in the morning. I felt important, not only to others, but also to myself. I was an actress! Even my boss commented on my more upbeat personality.

The acting classes led me to dream about writing and performing a one-woman show. After I saw Spaulding Grey perform his solo show, "Monster-in-the Box," I wanted to do a monologue, too. Mine would be about learning to love myself.

The opportunity presented itself in 2014, when a local theater group formed in town. The director and producer put out a call for actors, actresses, and playwrights. I showed up with my script and read it in front of a group of strangers. It even contained an a capella section where I sang a few lines from The Beatles' "Eleanor Rigby."

The director loved it. She suggested a few enhancements, which I agreed made it a stronger monologue. She called it "A Relationship with Me."

My fear of forgetting my lines never materialized. I performed the monologue to rave reviews and crossed another line off my "lead a kickass life" bucket list.

Looking back, I can't understand why I spent my early adulthood in a state of suspended animation. For ten years, I felt I had nothing to do when in reality I had everything to do.

Now, I wake up wondering if there will be enough time in the day to check out everything I want to explore.

Usually, there isn't. But, it's okay. I go to bed excited to wake up the next day and continue following my heart's desire.

# Way #24 Insight

Dive into all life has to offer. Explore. Experience. Expand.

~

# Monologue Tool Kit

**Song:** "Don't Rain on My Parade" (Message: Live Now.)
Artist: Barbara Streisand

**Movie:** *Monster in a Box* (1992). Spalding Gray performs a witty and insightful monologue about his psychological journey to write the monster, a 2,000-page semi-autobiographic novel about life after his mother's suicide.

**Book:** *Exhibit A: Short Plays and Monologues* by Neil Labute. Develop your acting chops by practicing with these short scripts.

**Activity:** Show up for a casting call at a local community theater.

# Brilliant Way #25

# Dare To Love

*"We are most alive when we're in love."* ~ *John Updike*

DURING HIGH SCHOOL, I worked part-time in a cheese shop on a farm. Every summer and fall, different local boys were hired to work in the fields or in the milk barn.

One of the new boys, Tim, regularly stopped in to watch me wield the sharp, double-handed blade to slice fifteen-pound wheels of Wisconsin cheddar into small wedges. I used my entire 110-pounds to seesaw the blade through the cheese wheel's heavily waxed exterior.

My slicing skills must have impressed him because in August Tim invited me to attend a concert in Boston. A group of his friends were going, some with dates, some without. I wore a miniskirt, a chocolate-brown turtleneck, dangling gold hoops, and lots of black eyeliner. His father picked me up at my home and dropped us off at the commuter rail, which we took into the city.

The band was awesome. The date was okay.

Tim's friends immediately started teasing me about wearing a turtleneck in the summer. "Aren't you dying in there?" Sure, I was burning up under the wool, but I was a crazy teen who thought she looked ravishing. Couldn't I do my own thing without being called out for it?

On the way home, Tim's friends kept pushing the back of our train seat until it flipped onto us. We kept moving and they kept following. Their adolescent behavior made it difficult to converse with my date.

I was mentally exhausted by the time Tim's father picked us up at the train station. "Thank you for a nice evening!" I yelled as I bolted toward my house.

A few days later, his father came into the cheese shop looking for Tim.

"Who's Tim?" I asked, failing to recognize the man that had driven us to and from the train station.

He gave me a weird look and left. Then it clicked who he was. Tim never stopped in again. But the minute I metaphorically pushed Tim away, via his dad, I decided that I liked him, after all.

Unfortunately, it was too late. Tim wanted nothing to do with me.

This push and pull became a hallmark of my dating patterns. If the guy liked me, I pushed him away; and if he didn't like me, I pulled him closer.

My inability to get close to anyone caused me a lot of anguish in my twenties and thirties. I thought I'd never find anyone I could love who would love me back. A work colleague told me, "It will be easy when you find the right guy." But my relationship future looked bleak.

Then a friend fixed me up on a blind date with her boyfriend's friend.

On the night of our date, Jimmy, an architect, greeted me with a wide smile, dark, sparkling Greek eyes, and a sweet hug. We strolled around my neighborhood, eating chocolate kisses while he pointed out historical architecture.

"That's a brick Richardson Romanesque with a hipped roof with multi-gabled dormers. Over there is a Second Empire with a mansard roof."

At the end of our date, he kissed me goodbye on the cheek.

My work friend was right. Dating Jimmy was easy. He loved doing everything with me: hiking in the White Mountains, cheering me at karaoke, helping me repaint my bedroom. We never broke up, or even threatened to break up. Each date was better than the one before.

Four years later, as we took a quick Christmas Eve nap on my bed, he slipped an engagement ring on my finger, got down on his knees, and asked me to marry him.

Without hesitation, I said, "Yes."

Finding love with Jimmy has been one of the great liberations of my life. He has seen the good, the bad, and the ugly of me. He has held my hand while I wept over a lost pet and laughed by my side in a Budapest traffic jam. He has argued with me over the best way to load the dishwasher.

In my earlier days, I was afraid of love, afraid that I wasn't worthy of it and that I couldn't return it. To stay safe, I picked men who mirrored that view of myself.

But none of that was true. I found love when I let down my guard long enough to receive it.

# Way #25 Insight

If you want to find love, let down your emotional guard. Love needs to be tended with vulnerability if you want it to grow.

~

# Dare To Love
# Tool Kit

**Song:** "Somebody to Love" (Message: Be active and find somebody to love.) Artist: Jefferson Airplane

**Movie:** *Something New* (2006). Loves knows no color.

**Book:** *The Mastery of Love: A Practical Guide To The Art of Relationship* by Don Miguel Ruiz. The road to love with another is paved with self love.

**Activity:** If you are single, ask someone out on a date. If you are married, ask your partner out on a date.

# Brilliant Way #26

# Don't Miss The Trip

*"There's no destination. The journey is all there is,
and it can be very, very joyful." ~ Srikumar Rao*

IN 2008, MY HUSBAND Jimmy and I biked across Italy for
twelve days with an adventure tour company. I've never done
anything as hard or as rewarding.

To be honest, the 363-mile trip was a bit out of our
physical league.

I'd signed us up after reading *A Walk in the Woods*, Bill
Bryson's hilarious tale about hiking the 2,500-mile Appalachian Trail. At first I wanted to do that six-month trek,
then Jimmy reminded me he only had a two-week vacation.

"We have to do something 'big' before we die," I pleaded.
"How about pedaling across Italy?"

"It's really mountainous. What about Holland?" he bargained.

"Too flat. We won't be challenged."

And challenged we were as we pedalled across the spine of Italy.

Despite training for the ride for five months before we left, we were the most out-of-shape folks on the trip.

Everyone else had run marathons, completed triathlons, extreme skied, and looked awesome in spandex.

Jimmy was twenty-five pounds overweight and I was a waif woman with minimal muscle.

On the first day, we struggled up the small warm-up hill to the point we were huffing and puffing and huffing. I feared we'd spend the entire "trip of a lifetime" cuddled up with the luggage in the sag wagon that followed us from place to place.

We quickly discovered the competitive nature of our buff fellow riders. They raced with one another from one Italian hilltop village to the next, always signing up for the extra fifteen-mile loop.

Unable to keep up with these Lance Armstrong wannabes, we consistently biked alone, arriving at the lunch spot when everyone else was leaving and at the hotel when everyone else was returning from the wine tasting.

One evening on our way back from a gelato place where Jimmy had shared all the gorgeous pictures he'd stopped and taken, one of the couples whispered, "Can we ride back with you tomorrow? We want to slow down long enough to see something."

They stayed with us for about two hours. Then took off to do the extra loop.

Jimmy and I may have always arrived last, but we saw the up-close-and-personal Italy the others breezed by.

We stopped often to take pictures of the tumbling landscape, the stone farmhouse architecture, the grazing animals, and the sun-weathered people.

As we took a breather in front of a sheep farm, the farmer came out and beckoned us into the large stone barn. He urged us to drink some kind of concoction from a long tube.

Best wine we ever had.

Halfway through the trip, the hill we pedaled up had become so steep I couldn't even stay on my bike. I got off to push it up the remaining 500 feet, when I turned around to get some sunscreen out of my pack.

A panoramic view of our long journey over rugged terrain greeted me. The life of yesterday I never saw because the push was always to move into tomorrow.

That awe-inspiring moment woke me up to the point of the trip, which wasn't to bike across Italy, but to feel across Italy, a land awash in taste, touch, sound, smell, and sight. My idea to do something "big," transformed into experiencing all the tiny "smalls" that strung together to create the big.

On the last day, when we reached the Mediterranean Sea and gathered for a final group photo with our back wheels in the water, I felt proud that an "out-of-shape" couple had not only physically biked across Italy, but also spiritually and emotionally traversed this mesmerizing land of my ancestors.

And unlike some of our "get-to-the-end" colleagues, we've got the pictures and tiny memories to prove it.

# Way #26 Insight

*Step out of the rush and appreciate the journey while you're on it.* We're taught at a young age to keep pushing to the next level to the point we forget how to enjoy the level we are currently at. As it has been said, "stop and smell the roses."

~

# Don't Miss The Trip Tool Kit

**Song:** "Gotta Love The Ride" (Message: The ride itself is paradise.) Artist: Mr. Big

**Movie:** *The Wizard of Oz* (1939). Young girl gets caught in a tornado and ends up in the world on the other side of the rainbow. While trying to get back home she makes new friends and learns lessons about what matter in life.

**Book:** *On the Road* with Jack Kerouac. Energetic adventure across America with the leader of the '60s Beat Generation.

**Activity:** Take a microscopic trip into your backyard. Get down on your hands and knees and really look at the tiny world around you.

# Lend A Helping Hand

*"You have not lived today until you have done something
for someone who can never repay you." ~ John Bunyan*

IN MY YOUTH, I was the center of my own universe.

I grew up in an affluent suburb, got whatever I asked for,
and never gave a thought to anyone less fortunate.

But I wasn't happy. Something was missing.

During my first professional job after college, I went to
lunch at a neighboring restaurant with some of my colleagues.
One day after I grabbed my sandwich and tossed the cashier
a five, my colleague Lisa turned to me and said, "Do you
know you never say 'thank you' to the folks who make your
sandwiches?"

Her remark stopped me in my self-centered tracks.

"No, I didn't," I said.

Clearly, other people were not on my radar, especially people that I had been trained to believe were socially beneath me.

Believe it or not, that one incident shook me to the core about my condescending ways. I vowed to be more grateful for what I had and to help those in need.

I took a five-week class at the library to become a literacy tutor in order to help immigrants from around the world speak better English. I participated in the annual City Year volunteer day and painted a bathroom at a mental health center. I escorted athletes back and forth off the field at the Special Olympics.

A few days after a snow storm, I was delivering groceries to a disabled senior when I noticed a frail older woman trying to take two feet of snow off her roof.

"Let me help you do that," I said using my gloved hands to remove the stacked powder.

With tears running down her face, she said, "Thank you. It isn't easy being eighty-four."

Every day provides opportunities to lend someone a helping hand. You can choose to formally volunteer or keep your eyes open for anyone struggling to survive.

For instance, one Saturday while taking my comforter into the laundromat to drop off for a cleaning, I noticed a woman in her late sixties get out of a rusting Chevy Lumina seemingly held together with grey electrical tape. She limped towards the building juggling a large, green trash bag filled with clothes and two bottles of detergent and fabric softener.

Her demeanor broke my heart.

I returned the next day with a Christmas gift certificate for $100 and asked the staff to give it to her. A few days later they called to say she'd left me a card.

It had an angel on the outside and inside she had written, "To my special Christmas angel, I don't know how you know me, but I am very grateful. Thank you." For the next three years, I gave her an anonymous Christmas gift.

In the end, lending others a helping hand fulfilled me in ways I never could have imagined.

When I started to focus on others, I achieved the inner peace and strength that had eluded me earlier in life. All because a friend had the courage to point out a shortcoming.

# Way #27 Insight

It's easier to find that elusive inner peace when you stop focusing on yourself and start focusing on others.

~

# Lend A Helping Hand Tool Kit

**Song:** "Helping Hand" (Message: What can you do to help someone?) Artist: Amy Grant

**Movie:** *Pay It Forward* (2000). Young boy is given a social studies assignment to improve the world. He decides to do good deeds for others in the hope they will pay it forward and do good deeds for others.

**Book:** *The Go Giver* by Bob Burg. In this fictionalized story, we follow the main character Joe as he discovers for himself the positive benefits of giving.

**Activity:** Sign up to be a volunteer for an organization whose mission you believe in.

# Brilliant Way #28

# Begin Anywhere

*"The secret to rich life is to have more beginnings than endings." ~ David Weinbaum*

MANY PEOPLE DON'T HAVE the courage to begin the things they really want to do.

Sure, they'll begin something that falls into the default "living" category, like shopping for a new flat-screen TV. But the juicy things that will free them from some captured element of themselves—those can be hard to begin. They involve the increasingly rare "go for it" attitude and the difficult leap of faith.

Unfortunately, the ability to trust ourselves to set our own course in life has been repressed. In some of us, it's so well hidden that we can't even find it within ourselves.

The good news: It's still there.

You just need gentle coaxing to take that first step on what Chinese philosopher Lao Tzu called "the journey of a thousand miles."

We all have many fears about taking that first step: We'll disappear into journey quicksand, we'll get lost in the unknown mist, we'll be scared once we leave the beaten path.

To me, those fears are the point.

I don't know where I'm going, and as scared as I may be, I know that to feel alive I need to step into the unknown, embracing its cool and unforgettable adventure.

Take my current painting process: I paint layers and layers of paint until it feels right. Then I step back and stare at the painting from different angles to see what wants to be born.

But it wasn't always that way.

I used to be a traditional painter, copying from photos. That was the model I learned in all my painting programs: Paint with the end in mind. So, whenever I picked up a brush, I was afraid my final product might not match the original.

Then I got the crazy idea to offer a program called "Wild Expressive Painting." The problem was, I didn't have any paintings that could be considered wild. Even when I tried to create one, my approach was cautious: a carousel horse that had freed itself from the carousel. It felt a bit tame, so I kept going.

Using watercolors, I quickly painted a loose dress from my imagination, a vivid swirl of color and movement? Some description? I called it "The Disobedient Wedding Dress."

I posted the image online, accompanying the description of my class; and within two days the class was full.

I kept experimenting in my art, and before I knew it, I had developed the wild expressive painting method I shared with the people in my program. No longer do I worry about making mistakes when copying from an original, the way I was trained. Now I paint unique scenes that don't have to look like anything but themselves.

Yet even now, I sometimes find myself thinking that I'm just wasting expensive paint and canvas on a colorful mess of nothingness. And it's usually at that pivotal moment, right before I give up, that I see the image lurking in the shapes and shadows. That's what I develop, trusting that I'm going in the right direction.

I could never simply pick up a paintbrush and consciously create the paintings I end up with.

I became a wild, expressive painter, creating truly original work that I love—all because I came up with a program title and needed the physical goods to back up my claim.

Can you imagine a world filled with people of all ages following their dreams and strengths?

The energy, enthusiasm, and excitement would be palpable. That world would be a more upbeat place with less depression and anxiety.

But the idea of moving to their own beat scares people whose life experiences have made them fearful. That trepidation to start something new gets ingrained in our psyches, until we can't do anything without seeking permission from some authority outside of ourselves.

The end result is a fear to take charge of our own lives, with far too many people spending their entire adulthood waiting for permission to start living the lives they truly desire. It becomes a circle with no entry, because the decision makers do not follow us through life.

How to get out of this trap? First, be aware of your own tendency to seek permission from others. Scribble down a list of things you want to start doing. Pick one small thing and take a tiny step toward it, then another …

# Way #28 Insight

In elementary school, we all learned to ask permission from others before doing what we wanted. Break out of that ingrained thinking. Give yourself permission to do what you want.

~

# Begin Anywhere
# Tool Kit

**Song:** "I Can See Clearly Now" (Message: Pick yourself up.)
Artist: Johnny Nash

**Movie:** *Norma Rae* (1987). A single mother takes on the difficult and dangerous mission to organize a union at the factory where she works and finds her purpose in the process.

**Book:** *Take Back Your Power* by Yasmin Davidds. Davidds sheds light on the learned ways we give away our power and provides methods to get it back.

**Activity:** Sign up for an activity that intrigues you. Do not let yourself cancel as the date gets closer.

# Brilliant Way #29

# Perseverance

*"When you get into a tight place, and everything goes against you till it seems you couldn't hold on a minute longer, never give up then, for that's just the place and time that the tide will turn."* ~ *Harriet Beecher Stowe*

WHEN I SET MY sights on something, I take a personal vow not to give up.

Most of the time, whatever I want to happen does indeed occur. But only because I didn't give into that human tendency to "run back to mommy" at the slightest bump in the road.

But first, let me be honest.

I used to throw up my hands in fake disgust and give up easily. I let jobs slip away, boyfriends, hobbies, even happiness.

It's clear to me now that I didn't really want those things, or I didn't want to fight for them. Because with a bit more determination and grit, they would have been mine to keep.

How do we get the gumption to persevere? First, decide what you truly want. Then be willing to do almost anything (legal) to get it.

When I first started writing, I got rejections. Lots of them. But I knew I had stories to tell, and I was determined to be published—and get paid for it. I tossed those rejections in the trash and kept writing.

After a few years of cold rejections, I began receiving warmer ones, often including personal notes: "If we had room for one more essay, it would have been this one." Or, "This essay wasn't quite right, but please send us any more you might have."

Eventually, my essays were published.

Sometimes editors emailed me promptly with acceptances. Other times, I received no response and had to follow up. When I did, some editors didn't want my essays after all. More often, though, my submission had simply gotten lost, or the editor had been sidetracked by other things. Once, an editor responded, "I love the essay, but we just published one on the same topic. Can you send it back in a year?"

Did I wait around? You bet I did. I wanted my writing in that publication, so I waited the year and sent it in again. The editor published it three weeks later.

Editors were the gatekeepers of my dreams. In this instance, only they could decide to pay me for my writing. Once I learned how busy they were, I became more confident about following up with them.

Who (or what) is the gatekeeper of your dreams? Is it a college admissions officer? The boss whose permission you need for time off? Or maybe the interior voice that tells you your dreams aren't worth the effort? Don't be put off, even by yourself. Follow up.

Many people give up just before they achieve the glorious thing they wanted. Maybe they can smell success, and back off out of fear. Perhaps they've run out of steam and have nothing left to give. Or maybe they don't really want it badly enough.

Don't let that happen to you. Decide what you want in life, and be willing to fight for it until you get it. I can almost guarantee that if you persevere, you can achieve anything your heart desires.

# Way #29 Insight

If you truly want something, command yourself to go after it until you get it. But be forewarned: As you get closer to the prize, you may try to talk yourself out of it.

~

# Perseverance Tool Kit

**Song:** "The Climb" (Message: When it gets tough, the tough get going.) Artist: Miley Cyrus

**Movie:** *Rocky* (1976). Struggling boxer gets an unexpected opportunity to fight the heavyweight champion of the world. Rocky prepares himself by training harder than he thought possible.

**Book:** *Unbroken* by Laura Hillenbrand. Moving story of one man's determination to survive, first in the Pacific Ocean for forty-seven days, later in a prisoner-of-war camp for three years.

**Activity:** Restart something you gave up.

# Brilliant Way #30

# Live Unscripted

*"Respond to every call that excites your spirit."* ~ *Rumi*

DESPITE ALL THE HIGH school and college commencement speeches encouraging graduates to go for the brass ring, most of them never grab it.

There's a problem with these speeches: Almost everything leading up to them has often countered their message of living a bold, daring life.

Those speeches wouldn't be needed if we encouraged young people to take chances all along, rather than telling them to play it safe by checking all the right boxes for college and career readiness. The experience of youth would be totally different if adults advised teens to bushwhack their own path through life instead of jumping on the "do it like everyone else" trail. Those inspirational commencement speeches often seem more like reminders for the adults who give them: Take risks before it is too late. (*Note to speaker self.*)

Most of our adult lives are far too scripted and safety-oriented.

If we saw our lives as an adventure, we'd embark on the next phase without worry, understanding that something even better was on the horizon. Or we'd step up and create it. New businesses exist only because someone takes a chance and creates one. If we don't raise people to do that, there won't be new small businesses that turn into larger ones.

When I got laid off after the 9-11 economic downturn, I cried myself a river of self-pity because I thought I'd never get another job. Two months later, I decided to make the leap and open my own business. It was hard at first to overcome the "play it safe" training I'd learned at school and work, but over time I developed my entrepreneurial muscles and attracted many wonderful clients.

While it's reasonable to take precautions like wearing seatbelts and driving the speed limit, it's clear that no matter how "safe," we try to make our lives, bad things may still happen, something my husband calls "the price of admission to life."

Too much concern with safety can make people start to curl in on themselves, terrified of taking even the tiniest risks. Yes, your life is as safe as you can make it; but is it the life you want to live?

Even knowing about the over focus on safety, I, too, still need to prevent myself from making my own life too safe. Like others, I feel the learned pull to safety all the time, and often start talking myself out of doing new things. (That's when I read myself the riot act and do something contrarian.)

For example, at a karaoke night, I decided to sing Barbara Streisand's "The Way We Were," a song I'd only heard two days before while watching the movie of the same name. My rendition started out okay, but two minutes into my performance, the lyrics began appearing onscreen two to three seconds after I needed to sing them. Instead of throwing my hands up in failure and sitting down with a pout, I improvised my way through it, making up words and, at times, even rhythms.

Things don't always go as planned, and that's fine with me. Okay, your turn.

How safe is your life? Do you like it safe, or do you yearn for a little more dangerous living? You may or may not. If you do, what one new thing can you try this week? It can be very small, like trying a new art technique; or it can be big, like hiking a 5,000-foot peak.

# Way #30 Insight

A more unpredictable, risk-taking life makes it easier to reignite your inner spark.

~

# Live Unscripted
# Tool Kit

**Song:** "Come Sail Away" (Message: Keep pursuing your dreams.) Artist: Styx

**Movie:** *The Year of Living Dangerously* (1982). Romantically involved journalist and embassy staffer dodge political unrest during the eve of a 1965 coup in Indonesia. Their feelings for each other heighten as violence erupts all around them.

**Book:** *The Joy of Living Dangerously* by Osho. Worry less about what people think of you and more about what you think of you. Then follow your own heart into the unknown.

**Activity:** What unexpected way can you alter your routine this week?

Self-Hope

# Words Of Encouragement

*"Stay close to anything that makes
you glad you are alive." ~ Hafiz*

CONGRATS ON FINISHING THE book and reigniting your
own spark!

I hope that after perusing it, listening to the suggested
songs, reading the recommended books, watching the suggested movies, and engaging in the proposed actions that
you are more in love with your life than before you started.

Since I've experienced the opposite way to go through
life, I can say without hesitation that I now have the life I've
imagined. No matter what anyone tells you, it is possible to
have your cake and eat it, too.

I choose to feel as alive as possible and wish the same
for you.

If this book has changed your life for the better, please consider sending me an email.

I'd love to hear all about it.

Thank you!

Giulietta "Julie" Nardone
giulietta@giuliettanardone.com
www.giuliettanardone.com

# Acknowledgments

*"At times our own light goes out and is rekindled by a spark from another person. Each of us has cause to think with deep gratitude of those who have lighted the flame within us."* ~ *Albert Schweitzer*

MY OWN FLAME HAS been rekindled by the sparks of everyone and everything I've come in contact with during my wild and crazy adventure through life. Glad to have spent precious moments with all of you.

Special gratitude to my dad Al, my mother Marilyn, my stepmother Fay, my mother-in-law, Anne, my sister, Joanne, my sister-in-law, Tina, and all my other family and friends.

Over the past twenty years, I've studied with many talented writing mentors, each one boosting me to the next writing level. Leigh Ann Henion and Kate Haas, you showed me how to write for the big leagues! I am forever grateful for your encouragement, edits, and enthusiasm. Kate, thank you for being the most fabulous beta reader. Your terrific suggestions helped shape *Feel More Alive* into the book of my self-hope dreams.

I also would like to thank my insightful publisher and co-collaborator Penelope Love of Citrine Publishing. Within five minutes of talking with you on the phone, I knew you were the perfect messenger for *Feel More Alive!* You've been a true partner every magical step of the way.

And, Jimmy, love of my life. You gave me the support, time, and space to write a book about living a brilliant life. I am forever grateful.

# About The Author

Giulietta nardone is an inspirational writer, painter and singer living in Massachusetts with her husband and two frolicsome cats. She leads imagination and creativity programs in person and online, and gives "magical" talks with her imperfect, unforgettable voice.

*www.giuliettanardone.com*

# Publisher's Note

THANK YOU FOR READING *Feel More Alive!* Please pass the torch of connection by helping other readers find this book. Here are suggestions for your consideration:

+ Write an online customer review
+ Gift this book to friends, family, and colleagues
+ Share a photo of yourself with the book on social media and tag #giuliettanardone and #inspirationasmedicine
+ Bring in Giulietta Nardone as a speaker for your business, club or organization
+ Suggest *Feel More Alive!* to your local book club, and download the Book Club Discussion Questions from our website: www.citrinepublishing.com/bookclubs
+ For bulk orders, contact the publisher at (828) 585-7030 or email orders@citrinepublishing.com
+ Submit a story for the *Feel More Alive!* Writing Contest: www.giuliettanardone.com/fma-writing-contest/

Your book reviews, shares and letters are received with our open arms, gratitude, and a resounding *"How fantastic!"*

CPSIA information can be obtained
at www.ICGtesting.com
Printed in the USA
JSHW021128221020
8965JS00004B/68